Temple Beth David
6100 Hefley Street
Westminster, CA 92683
(714) 892-6623

Strangers in Their Own Land

STRANGERS IN THEIR OWN LAND

Young Jews in Germany
and Austria Today

PETER SICHROVSKY

TRANSLATED BY JEAN STEINBERG

Basic Books, Inc., Publishers   New York

Library of Congress Cataloging-in-Publication Data

Sichrovsky, Peter, 1947–
Strangers in their own land.

Translation of: Wir wissen nicht was morgen wird, wir
wissen wohl was gestern war.
1. Children of Holocaust survivors—Germany (West)—
Biography. 2. Children of Holocaust survivors—
Austria—Biography. 3. Jews—Germany (West)—Biography.
4. Jews—Austria—Biography. I. Title.
DS135.G5A1613   1986   943'.004924   85-43108
ISBN 0-465-08211-4

For my grandparents
whom I will never forget
although I never knew them.

For my parents
who survived
and had the courage
to return and begin again.

CONTENTS

ACKNOWLEDGMENTS

I WANT to thank all the men and women whom I interviewed for their kindness and patience in talking with me about their lives. I especially thank my friend Ronny Scheer of Vienna, who for many years has tried to remind me of my roots and who assisted me in preparing the Austrian material.

New York
November 1985

Strangers in Their Own Land

Introduction

SOME BOOKS are inspired by the most bizarre situations. The idea can come to a writer anywhere: in a theater, while skiing, or while dining with friends. A seemingly insignificant allusion, a remark, a partially overheard conversation at the adjacent table, the face of a man seen on an escalator, can set off a spark that months or years later will ignite a book.

But that was not the case here. This book grew out of my own development over a period of many years. It was intended to answer or help find the answer to one particular question: What does it mean for me as a Jew to live in Germany today? And related to that question was my curiosity about how others in a like situation are answering it.

Until the age of thirty I was not concerned with problems such as Jewish identity or the life of Jews in Germany and Austria. But lately these matters have become increasingly important, to the point where they are crucial factors in my life.

And the question about life as a Jew here in Germany or Austria has given rise to a wealth of other questions. Who were the people who returned? Who are the ones who want to stay here? How do those who want to stay here live, and where do those who want to leave go? How did the experiences of the parents affect the children, my generation? How do they, the children of the survivors, cope with the German and Austrian environment? How do the children of the killers live together in the same country with the children of the victims?

These are not theoretical questions; my own situation has forced me to confront each of them. As the son of surviving Jews, I was familiar with Austria and Germany. I had grown up in the former and have been living in the latter for the past few years.

Since moving to Berlin in particular, I have been looking for people who share my situation. I have joined various Jewish groups and organizations that have put me in touch with Jews of my generation. I sought them out and soon realized that we shared a concern with two central themes: first, the problem of a resurgent racism, combined with the complex reaction to our gruesome past; and second, the question of whether, given the way we felt, we ought to stay here or leave. These themes are being discussed within Jewish groups with an enormous degree of emotional intensity. At the same time it is obvious that in our contact with non-Jews, with the "other" Germans and Austrians, these topics are hardly ever touched on.

As time went on I was struck by the fact that we Jews in Germany and Austria live a double life. On the one hand we present a nearly unmarred apparently problem-free façade. On the other hand our inner life fluctuates between fear and aggression. It is a life marked by the experiences of our parents and other relatives, but this side is revealed only to other Jews.

INTRODUCTION

Recently, a non-Jewish German woman attended a gathering of Jewish intellectuals in Berlin. Her presence made the Jews uneasy. Since they were not just among themselves, they could not speak freely. They felt that they were being observed.

What I wanted to do was break through the wall built around the Jews of my generation in Germany and Austria. I set out to look for people who would share their feelings with me. My subjects had to meet the following criteria: they had to be Jews born after 1945, and they had to have lived in Austria or Germany for at least ten years. My conversations with them turned out to be very difficult. Many of them were talking about their feelings for the first time, while others had been arguing about the subject for years and had ready-made theories and interpretations. But in the course of time I found an approach that generally made my subjects responsive. Rather than handing them a questionnaire, I began with my own story, telling them about my parents and grandparents and about my own life. Giving them the feeling they were talking to someone with similar problems was a crucial factor.

And so most of them opted for the historical method, and working their way up to the present, they talked about their ancestors and what had happened to them. Only a few were able to talk freely about their lives as Jews in Germany or Austria, however. Often it became extremely seductive to take refuge in analyses and theories, to talk about the problem of Jews and anti-Semitism in general and to steer clear of the personal situation. But I was interested in the small events: the first day of school, the first love, everyday experiences, the worries and concerns of the often ridiculous incidents of daily life. I kept at it, questioning and trying to stir memories of forgotten or seemingly unimportant events. Fifty preliminary talks were followed by twenty-five longer interviews, of which thirteen are included here. The briefest of these interviews lasted almost three hours, the longest one an entire week during which I spent a few hours each day with the subject. The typed interviews ran to some one thousand pages. The talks as they appear here are not transcripts of those interviews. I have tried to boil them down into portraits of the people whom I interviewed, and that wasn't always simple. I have condensed, shortened, even changed the emphasis of their words, but I have never altered the meaning of anything that was said. Nonetheless some of them retracted their interviews after reading them, either because they were alarmed to read what they had said or because they didn't want to hurt their families. Others were afraid—afraid that their neighbors would recognize them, that their children would suffer in school. And some simply had an undifferentiated fear, a nagging malaise. For Jews to speak openly about the feelings growing out of life in Germany or Austria just isn't all that simple.

Although I found some striking differences among the reactions of the people I interviewed, I found even greater similarities. The past lived on very strongly in all of them, but the vast majority of the families hardly ever talked about the Nazi horrors; or the answers to questions about the past were tears. In this they resemble the families of former Nazis. Here, too, we hear the children complain that their parents don't tell them anything. In an article about this problem I came across this sentence: In the house of the hangman there is as little talk about the rope as there is talk about the dead in the house of the victims.

Even if the motives of the different families vary, the fact that those Jewish parents who survived the Nazi terror are reluctant to speak of it is bound to affect the self-confidence of the next generation, above all with regard to the problem of Jewish identity. My generation has frequently been forced to reconstruct the events of that time for themselves out of casual references and remarks. Here we find differences between those parents who were in concentration camps and those who survived in emigration. The worse their experiences, the less likely they are to speak about them, and the more difficult it was for me to find an avenue of approach to their children and to induce the young people to talk about themselves.

In the final analysis all who agreed to have their stories appear here violated a taboo. They overcame strong inhibitions about discussing their experiences and telling these stories outside their Jewish environment. Ordinarily these young Jews put on a mask when dealing with others; only when they are among themselves do they allow themselves to remove that mask. They revealed themselves in order that the generation of new Germans and Austrians, as well as the older people, might become aware that a new generation of Jews is living here for whom the past is not dead. These young Jews are deeply distrustful and filled with doubts. For them the horrors of the Holocaust cannot be wiped out with a few well-turned phrases, but live on in a generation that cannot and does not want to forget them.

German TV likes to show pictures of tearful older people returning from abroad to spend their last years in their old homeland. Again and again they say—and the audience eats it up—that they harbor no feelings of vengeance. But every time I see this sort of thing, I have the urge to shout out, "You out there, you don't have the faintest idea what these people say when they are among themselves!"

A young journalist told me after reading excerpts of my manuscript that he was profoundly shaken, not so much by the feelings, thoughts, and experiences brought to light as by his own ignorance. He had thought that because of his personal contacts with Jews he knew them. He had no idea, and his conversations with his Jewish friends gave no clue, that this generation of Jews was still so affected by the experiences of their parents. He tried to explain his reaction in this way:

Suppose you've been seeing somebody regularly for years, and you think you know that person pretty well. To judge by the way he looks, by his friendly demeanor, you believe him to be more or less happy, like you yourself. But one day you go to the beach with him, and for the first time you see him stripped. Looking at his naked body you recoil, for he is covered with scars from head to toe.

1

Fritz

A Conflict of Head and Heart

IF, as is often said, we children of the Jews who survived suffer from a delayed reaction, I must be a prime exhibit, for my parents survived here, inside Germany. Yes, here, not in some camp, but right here in Berlin, hiding out for almost five years. They didn't even know each other then. I could never quite picture it, and I still can't. While hundreds of thousands, even millions, of Jews were being hauled off, they were sitting in some kind of cubbyhole playing hide-and-seek with the Nazis, not reporting for any of the transports, those pseudo-vacation trips. In my imagination I can see it all, but the reality must have been very different. But my imagination—and that's all I have to go on, because neither my mother nor my father has really told me anything about that time—my imagination keeps on showing me strange double images. It's like a split screen. On the right there are the usual pictures of the Nazi era we see in the movies or on TV: the parades, the war, the mass hysteria, the outstretched arms, the occasional picture of a concentration camp. On the left side of the screen I see an entirely different picture: a room without a window, a single naked lightbulb partly covered with a cloth to keep the light to a minimum. Here I see my parents, just sitting or reading a book or staring at the ceiling or looking at me in the movie house watching them in the movie.

Before, when I was young, I didn't believe their story. There were all those who had died, in both my mother's and my father's family. Then there were those few who were able to escape, and the still fewer ones who survived the camps. But to just hide out here in Berlin! I knew nobody except my parents who managed that. Even today I somehow catch myself doubting it. I have to learn to accept the unimaginable.

In the 1930s my mother, then a young girl, was working in the household of a wealthy Jewish family. Maybe she was their baby sitter, I don't know. Her father had come from the East— from Poland, I think—and somehow managed to scrape out a living here. As a child she knew hardly any German. Yiddish was spoken at home, and she was lucky to have gotten work with that particular family. One day, in 1939 or 1940, the people she worked for were taken away in the middle of the night. What happened then is pure Hollywood. While the Germans were busy carting the family off, my mother hid in a corner. She wasn't even missed, because she wasn't part of the family. My mother didn't dare leave the little room she was hiding in, coming out only at night to get some food from the kitchen. Then, after about three days, a new family moved in. I don't know who they were, my mother never mentioned their name. It was a couple with three older children. While the woman was making an inspection tour of the house, she discovered my mother. She kept her hidden for five years in the same house, in

A Conflict of Head and Heart

some corner in the attic where the son of the Jewish family had built a little private retreat for himself. The man, probably some sort of high official—how else would he have gotten this Jewish villa?—knew nothing. For five years he lived under the same roof with a Jewish woman, probably bragging to his cronies about his great house, now cleansed of Jews. The children knew, but they stuck with their mother and even helped her. That's all I know about the whole business. I eagerly snapped up any scrap of information my mother volunteered, but I never asked her what was really going on then. I couldn't say why. Probably because I didn't want to remind her of that time. My mother never saw either her parents or her sisters and brothers after the war. Some years later she received word from the Red Cross that they had been murdered in Auschwitz.

As far as my father is concerned I know even less about him. I think before the war he was involved in all sorts of shady business, not that I blame him. He wasn't a criminal, but the circles in which he moved were not exactly made up of upright, solid citizens. He and his family had also come from the East. He never told me what his father did for a living. His parents were also taken away, but when the Nazis came to get them my father wasn't at home. It happened in 1942, and from then until 1945 he lived underground in Germany, in hiding. He constantly had to change his hide-outs, living here and there, being helped by people who, as he put it, "had all, at one time or another, breathed reused air." But I was never told anything more specific. In answer to my questions he always said the same thing: "Somehow I survived, but even I couldn't tell you how."

I think, and I hope I'm not doing him an injustice by saying this, he did it by sheer chutzpah. He doesn't look very Jewish, what with his blond hair and pale-blue eyes. From remarks he dropped I gathered that he didn't pay any attention to the regulations, like wearing the Jewish star. He simply took his chances and moved around like any other ordinary German.

After the war my parents stayed here in Germany. They crawled out of their holes like coming out of an air-raid shelter. Just like that. They met shortly after the war and got married. But I can only guess at why they are living here in Germany. When I was about twelve or thirteen and beginning more and more to think about the Third Reich and the persecution of the Jews something strange happened. I don't think I'll ever forget it. One evening I was sitting watching TV with my parents. It was a documentary about the Nuremberg trials. No one said a word. The silence was deafening. When the program ended my father got up and turned the TV off. There was no way we could have listened to a commercial after that. Perhaps just to break the silence, and wanting to gauge the mood of my parents, I said, "They should have tried more of those swine. The Germans were and are a bunch of shits." Before I got the words out, my father grabbed me, pulled me up from the chair, and slapped my face. I think it's the only time he's ever hit me. "If, as you put it, all Germans were shits, neither your mother nor I would be standing here today. Never forget that." Those were his very words. That's how it was in our house. It's hard to believe, my father as the defender of the Germans. For him collective guilt, *the* Nazis, *the* fascists, but also *the* Germans, didn't exist; there was only individual guilt. With me it was entirely different. I didn't distinguish. I hadn't had any positive experiences, or negative ones either, and certainly not with older Germans, to show me that there were two kinds of Germans. When I talked with a German old enough to have experienced the Nazi era consciously, and it didn't happen very often, I always got the same answer: "Those were bad times. We were all aroused and didn't really want any of it. And we knew nothing about the

A Conflict of Head and Heart

persecutions and extermination camps." Always the same answers, particularly from my teachers. No one was guilty or talked
about personal guilt; no, all of them had been seduced and led
astray by a magical, hypnotizing force. Not a single one was
willing to say, "I was for the Nazis then and I'm still for them
now." I would have been happy to meet a single person who
would truthfully have said to me, "I was for carting the Jews
off and killing them because I hated them." But I
never heard that. Nothing. They were all innocent, like duped
children.

When I was fourteen or fifteen, I considered all older Germans a diffuse, undifferentiated mass of hypocrites, liars, and
unpunished murderers. I felt no hatred, because I couldn't focus
it on any one person. But in the papers I occasionally would see
pictures of some concentration camp guards or SS types. They
looked like anyone else, like my neighbor or the bus driver.
There was no one I could hate because he had been one of
them, not a single man, not a single woman. Perhaps that's why
I was such an aggressive child, particularly in my teens. I was
forever fighting with other children, and if someone in a bus
accidentally stepped on my foot and didn't apologize right away
I would call him an old Nazi swine.

I was a good student; perhaps I even enjoyed special privileges
in school. Apparently the anti-Semitism of the Nazis was followed by the guilty conscience of de-Nazification. When I got
into a fight, the others were punished more severely than I, and
if someone in my class complained about me, they would say
things like "You know how he is, what he's gone through," and
so on. I enjoyed this special treatment and even exploited it. In
school I never experienced any form of anti-Semitism. Perhaps I
was simply too aggressive, particularly toward my fellow students; they just didn't dare. And as far as the teachers were

concerned I was probably just plain lucky. Many of my friends, children of Jewish families, had bad experiences in school, even back then, soon after the war. And when their parents visited us, the topic was always the same: Was there any trouble? What happened to your son? What happened to your daughter? All I could tell them was that everybody left me alone. In that respect I was almost unique among my Jewish friends.

After graduating from high school I studied law. I had always wanted to be a lawyer—actually an odd decision for a Jew in Germany, helping Germans beat the law. I finished my studies in record time and now have my own law office, together with six partners. I am considered successful. I have money, I can move about freely in my convertible. I'm wealthy, respected, successful, a welcome guest at the parties of people who count. I can be said to have made it. Forty years after my extended family, a group of about two hundred, was reduced to five, I am once again permitted to move freely among Germans. But nothing I have here, whether it's my six-room apartment, my office, car, or stocks, means anything to me. The only reason I'm living here in Germany is my profession. I love this profession, probably above all because I'm practicing it here in Germany. I have an inexplicable sympathy for German criminals. I've never been analyzed, but I'm sure a psychiatrist would have a field day with me. What I like best of all is defending real criminals, all those thieves, murderers, swindlers, the worse the better. I like these types and their perversions. The nastier the better. Everything that does not spell decent German I find appealing, and I'd do anything in my power to defend these types. I certainly don't lack clients. Word has gotten around in certain circles that I'm a good defense lawyer.

Some months ago I had a particularly interesting case. Two juveniles had broken into the apartment of an elderly couple,

A Conflict of Head and Heart

tied them up, and robbed them. They gagged the seventy-year-old man, and he suffocated. Here the victims interested me more than the perpetrators. I had found out that the old man had been a high-ranking SS officer, and that some years earlier proceedings against him had been dropped. The prosecution witnesses—two old women who in giving their testimony before a German court broke down when asked to describe the slaughter of their relatives and friends—these witnesses did not appear credible to the German court. For me the defense of the two youthful criminals turned into a personal settling of accounts with the German judicial system. For weeks I prepared myself —I don't want to go into details here—but the work I put in was out of all proportion. In the end the case didn't go so badly for the defendants.

I would defend the worst crooks, regardless of whether they were able to pay me or not. My parents also approve of what I'm doing, especially my father. They lead very quiet lives, have few friends, and manage to get by. They're members of the Jewish Community but they're not very religious. Still, all their friends are Jews, including many who don't belong to the Community. I love my parents, and I'm very close to them. I cannot imagine life without them and dread the day when they will no longer be here. What I like best of all is arguing with my father. It's fun. My father is an impassioned CDU [Christian Democratic Union] supporter. He always says that the CDU is the party of the bigger scoundrels, but somehow he means it positively. Basically he is a pure cynic. He doesn't trust the Left. When Geissler drew a parallel between the peace movement and Auschwitz, my father said to me, "See, I told you. They're the bigger scoundrels." To this day I don't know exactly what he means by scoundrels, but he seems to divide the people here into Germans and scoundrels, and he clearly prefers the latter.

FRITZ

My mother is entirely different. She doesn't talk much about politics. Her greatest interest is the family. She's forever asking me how I'm doing, whether I have enough to eat, and above all she wants to know about my children.

Ten years ago, at age twenty-five, I got married. My wife is a lawyer. We occasionally work together. She's also Jewish. Her parents emigrated to the United States way back, and she returned to study here. Even though she grew up in America, she feels more at home here. Her parents can't understand it. I met them shortly before we got married. They had left Germany in 1934. Her father had been a member of the German Communist Party. They survived by a miracle. A day before they were scheduled to leave, they received an anonymous phone tip telling them that they were on the "list." They got to the United States by way of Austria, Switzerland, and France. They, too, survived through the help of a German. Both my wife's parents and my own were saved by Germans, by Germans who violated the law, who did not obey, who did not submit to official regulations, who risked their lives and the lives of those close to them. According to the law of that time, those who saved them were criminals. In the rest of the world they are heroes, but here in Germany they are unsung heroes.

My wife's parents stayed in the United States. They now live in New York. Her father is a professor of history. Her family leads a very traditional Jewish life, and both her parents are active in Jewish organizations. Their left-wing politics are a thing of the past.

They cannot understand why my parents stayed in Germany after the war. Once they even said that staying in Germany was tantamount to a betrayal of the dead. When their daughter went to Germany to study and we met and married, relations between daughter and parents suffered a serious blow. The parents said

A Conflict of Head and Heart

that there could be a resurgence of fascism, that by living here we were volunteering to put our asses on the line. They even went so far as to tell her not to have children here in Germany and under no circumstances to acquire German citizenship. By the way, she has remained an American citizen.

But lately things have quieted down. My parents-in-law have visited us; they have seen how we live and enjoy our children and our success. Still, whenever they read anything about neo-Nazi activities or German xenophobia, they call us up from New York to tell us that anytime we want we can pack up and move to the United States and they will help us get a fresh start.

In the meantime we have become the parents of two children and live like any other family. My wife works in the office of a friend of mine, mainly on problems of political refugees. Our life has been wonderful, but our wedding was a tragedy. We had dreamed of a traditional Jewish wedding, something we knew only from the movies or stories our parents told us, weddings with songs and dances and many relatives and friends. A few weeks before the planned festivities—my wife's parents had come over from America—we were sitting around a table making up the guest list, and only then did we realize how few of us were left. I'd never really been aware of it. When I was going to school I was surrounded by friends and classmates and had never felt lonely. True, I was something of a curiosity, one of only a handful, but there were all those others, and even though they were the others, they at least were there, as a backdrop, a noisy environment. Initially we had planned to invite only close relatives of our two families. We came up with a total of fifteen. It was a depressing evening. I'll never forget it. We sat down together to celebrate a feast of the survivors and it turned into reminiscences about the dead. One after the other was remembered by name: grandfather dead, grandmother dead, my father's two sisters dead, my mother's brother dead, uncles, aunts, cousins—all dead. Murdered in Auschwitz, in Theresienstadt, and who knows where else. Two families, and all we could come up with was fifteen close relatives. That evening, while planning the wedding, I realized for the first time the full extent of the madness that had reigned here. Instead of a happy gathering, the evening turned into a session filled with impotent anger, helpless despair, and mourning. We tried to make the best of the wedding and invited assorted friends and acquaintances. A hundred guests showed up, but they were an illusion, a paid audience, supernumeraries hired for the evening to lend an air of gaiety. Since that day I've known that here in Germany I belong neither to the majority, the Germans, nor to a minority, the Jews, because that minority no longer exists. We are a ridiculously small group, probably no more than twenty to thirty thousand in all of Germany. We are an infinitesimally small, odd collection of outsiders, and if we are seen at all it is only because of anti-Semitic remarks or because of the politics of Israel.

Sometimes even the outcry about the resurgence of anti-Semitism strikes me as ridiculous. Whom do they propose to protect or guard? That miserable handful of us? I'm always reminded of the appeals by societies for the preservation of endangered species. The Jews, no, we mustn't do anything to them, they've already suffered enough. What could still happen to us here? It wouldn't even pay to erect a special camp for us. More Jews perished in a single day's transport under the Nazis than are now living in the German Federal Republic. But today we are protected, cosseted, and pampered. Our synagogues are being renovated, at least those that haven't been turned into supermarkets. Jewish given names are *in*, above all among the Leftists, and vacations are spent in Israel. The decline of literature due to the absence of Jewish writers is regretted, and school

A Conflict of Head and Heart

children are forced to visit concentration camps. Compulsory, just like driver-education courses.

Recently I heard a charming Irish pop song on the radio. It is called "The Head and the Heart," and it contains this line: "It is the classical dilemma between the heart and the head." It tells of the love for a woman. The lyrics of this admittedly somewhat kitschy song aptly describe my relationship to Germany—a conflict of head and heart. With my head I belong here in Germany. Everything here is in working order. I am successful, respected, have plenty of money, and feel safe. I am told daily that nothing can happen to me here. We have a democracy, the Basic Law,* and we even have a few Jews sitting in the Federal legislature. But the heart, the heart remains unquiet. It beats restlessly, is nervous, often even fearful. With my heart I am not a German and never will be. And when I think that I shall be buried here in Germany, chills run down my spine. The bad part is that any discussion about this is bound to be inconclusive. Almost every conversation with my wife, my parents, or my friends ends with the question of whether to remain or to leave. And the head always wins out over the heart. I am here today and will still be here tomorrow. But if I stay here, I am sure to die of heart failure, because no heart can stand this sort of humiliation forever.

* The constitution of the German Federal Republic.

2

Michael and Anna

Our Children Are at Home Here

MICHAEL: My parents were not directly affected by the Holocaust. My grandparents, together with my father and his two sisters, had already emigrated to Palestine in 1933. Actually they had wanted to go to America, but that didn't work out because none of our relatives there was able to get the papers needed. My grandfather had been to Palestine once before, in 1925, and he hadn't really wanted to go there again, but he realized that it represented his last hope.

My grandparents lived in Berlin-Lichterfelde* and were relatively well-to-do. They owned a large house. My grandfather was an executive in an insurance company. At the end he was accused of financial hanky-panky. My father himself was often beaten up by anti-Semites. He was seventeen when he came to Palestine. He got a job in a metal-smelting plant, but the work was too hard for him. He was not used to heavy physical labor.

* A middle-class section of Berlin.

Our Children Are at Home Here

He then got a job as an auto mechanic in Tel Aviv and became a master mechanic. After fifteen years of hard work he opened his own shop, which he owns to this day.

My mother was born and grew up in Hildesheim.* Her parents died when she was eight years old, and she was raised by her grandmother. Both she and her grandmother left Germany in 1933. My grandmother had always wanted my mother to give up Judaism. She subscribed to the belief that the best solution for Judaism lay in its dissolution. Her goal was total assimilation. She enrolled my mother in a lyceum and hoped that she would marry a Christian. Yet despite her desire to become an ordinary German, she was shrewd enough to see the threatening catastrophe early on.

ANNA: Your mother is 150 percent German. To this day she doesn't really know any Hebrew. And she patronizes only stores where German is spoken.

MICHAEL: That's true. She lives in a small apartment in Tel Aviv furnished with all the stuff they brought with them from Germany.

ANNA: There are circles of emigrants who have remained Germans. They spend their vacations in Austria, Germany, or Switzerland. But they're slowly dying out. Many of the new generation often don't even know any German.

MICHAEL: But the Germans were the elite there in Israel. German workmanship was held in high regard. There was racial differentiation, beginning with the Germans on top down to the Arabs, the lowest level. The Germans brought European culture to the country. The Russians were the second elite, and as I see it they were subdivided into two groups. First there were those who had come before the October Revolution. They lived in beautiful, expensive houses and were also on a high cultural level, perhaps even higher than the Germans. Many of the big

* An industrial town in the vicinity of Hanover.

21

businesses in Israel belong to families from this group. The second Russian elite was composed of the Socialists and Communists, who brought socialist ideas to the Jewish workers. That collectivism later became the basis of the kibbutzim.

At any rate, I was born in Israel in 1945. I learned German from my parents and Hebrew in school. With my parents I spoke only German, and that often made for problems. When I spoke German with my mother in public we were often abused and criticized. "Why do you speak German with your child?" they would ask. Once we were even kicked off a bus. But my mother didn't care. She had a resonant voice that carried to all within earshot and she stuck by her right to speak German.

Also she never felt like a victim of persecution. Back in 1955 or '56, after the Adenauer–Ben-Gurion talks, when it became possible to reapply for German citizenship, she filed immediately.

ANNA: And even though Michael had never set foot in Germany, this automatically made him a German citizen.

MICHAEL: If not for that, we probably wouldn't be here today.

ANNA: That's right, because I still have my Israeli citizenship, and I don't intend to give it up.

MICHAEL: I also have Israeli citizenship. When we go to Israel in the summer I'm still on the army reserve list, and when I leave the country I need the permission of my military unit.

ANNA: Theoretically they could keep him there and make him serve three or four weeks. That's not exactly a pleasant thought.

MICHAEL: Okay, but they've never done it. Anyway, after finishing school I followed in my father's footsteps and learned his trade in his shop. Everything looked great at the time, and I never thought of leaving Israel. But with the war of 1973 everything changed. I was called up and served six months in the military, but I didn't like the political situation. A feeling of pessimism was spreading through the country. Also, I didn't want to go into business with my father because of his partner. Anna and I had the feeling that everything was disintegrating. We were expecting our first child, and more and more our thoughts turned toward Europe.

After the '67 war everyone had still been very optimistic. There was a feeling of euphoria in the country, things were being built, unemployment was nonexistent, and a great deal of restitution money was coming into the country. But then, five years later, everything suddenly began going to pieces. The bad part, as far as I was concerned, was that my faith in the army was shattered. That sacred army had been my idol. So we decided at first on a two-year trial period in Europe, a sort of learning vacation, away from the strains of life in Israel. We never intended to leave for good.

ANNA: And we still don't.

MICHAEL: First I went to Switzerland by myself, but I couldn't get a work permit. Finally I got a job near the German border and wrote to Anna to join me with the baby. I worked in a plant that makes trucks. The work was hard, but I learned a lot there.

ANNA: My father came to visit us once. He happened to be in Berlin for six months and advised us to come to Berlin, which we did.

MICHAEL: Then our second daughter was born. We've now been here for more than nine years. We've made some friends and have adjusted quite well, and we're satisfied. When we visit Israel in the summer it feels like home, and then again it doesn't. Our old friends have become strangers; we've grown apart.

ANNA: My mother was born in Berlin. Her parents came from Poland. My mother was never a German citizen. Her father was in the egg business, and theirs was a traditional Jewish household. They went to synagogue on the Sabbath and observed all the holidays, and all my mother's friends were Jewish. She knew about Zionism long before Hitler. Her older brother had gone to Palestine in the 1920s to help found a kibbutz. Two weeks before Kristallnacht,* her parents told her that this wasn't a good time for her to be here, and they sent her to Palestine.

They bought a ticket and sent her off alone, ahead of them, intending to follow her later. But the last time my mother saw her parents was at the train station in Berlin. My grandfather still corresponded with my mother until 1940. Always in Hebrew. She still has his letters. When you read these letters, you'd think that the man had been speaking Hebrew all his life. Her parents were later transported and murdered. Today my mother is a true Israeli. She speaks fluent Hebrew, is very spontaneous and warm. She says that Israel gave her back the identity the Germans took away from her. She likes living in Israel and cannot imagine living in Germany again for any length of time.

My father was born in Vienna in 1919. His father came from Prague, his mother from Poland. His father was in the pocketbook business in Vienna. His upbringing wasn't particularly traditional. He was a good student. He studied law, but his real interests were history and German language and literature, studies he was able to pursue only after twenty years in Israel, at Tel Aviv University. My father considered himself an Austrian first and a Jew second. In 1938 he was driven out of Vienna because he was a Jew. He emigrated to Jerusalem, where he had relatives, and they later also took in his parents. Emigration from Vienna, from Europe, from the German cultural sphere, was a shock that he still hasn't absorbed completely. On the other

* A pogrom organized by the Nazis against Jewish stores, businesses, and synagogues in Germany during the night of 10 November 1938. The event was called *Kristallnacht* (night of crystal) in reference to the broken glass that littered the streets.

hand, it made possible the realization of his dream to be a scholar.

In his early days in Palestine, my father supported himself and his parents by producing small leather goods. For the time being he had to set aside his dreams of German philology and history. Only many years later, with the help of my mother, when my brother and I were already sixteen and eighteen years old respectively, was he able to do something about it. He went to Germany and got a degree in history. As the founder and head of the German Institute at Tel Aviv University, he has gained renown as a historian.

When my mother was eighteen, she enrolled in an agricultural institute in Palestine. About two years later she moved to the city, trying her hand at various jobs to make a living. She earned her keep working as a kitchen maid and housekeeper. My parents met in German emigré circles and got married in 1945. As members of the Communist Party of the young state of Israel, they, like many others, were full of hope and optimism about the new state that arose after the Holocaust.

MICHAEL: In 1972 the first institute for the study of the German language, literature, and history was founded at Tel Aviv. It was the forerunner of today's German Goethe Institute. Despite its modest scope it became a center for German emigrants, who welcomed it enthusiastically. Anna and I met in a language course and we got married in 1973.

ANNA: My parents spoke German with each other but Hebrew with us children. After my military service my parents sent me to Germany so I could learn the language of the poets and thinkers and murderers.

MICHAEL: We've now lived in Berlin for more than nine years. Our daughters are completely integrated; we too feel comfortable, have a nice circle of friends. We have never experienced discrimination or anti-Semitism or anti-Jewish smears, even though the media have made us aware that these problems exist. We can see for ourselves that the hatred of foreigners, refugees, and colored peoples is on the rise. That's a strong reminder of the past, and we're now trying to sort out what it means for us.

ANNA: I've had more experience in this respect than Michael. He looks like a German and speaks without an accent. I have a pronounced foreign accent. When old people ask me where I'm from and I tell them that I'm from Israel, they immediately become defensive and tell me that they were innocent, that they hadn't known anything, and some also tell me that they had helped Jews. On the other hand I often hear older people say things like "In the old days this could never have happened," or "There was order then." I can't stand it and I get furious. I tend to react very aggressively and let them know how I feel. "We've all seen and experienced what this law and order led to," I yell at them.

MICHAEL: But there exists another, far more malicious, indirect form of anti-Semitism, and it is widespread. After the Israeli invasion of Lebanon these old types came to me, clapped me on the shoulder, and said, "What a great job you've done on the Arabs. You've shown the world what revenge is. Your army learned all that from our Adolf!"

I also won't forget the old man who came to me after the Entebbe incident and said, "You've done it again. That's exactly how we would have done it. Your army is as good as ours was."

They say these things to me without thinking, without blushing, convinced that they are complimenting me.

ANNA: On the other hand, when we see our friends in Israel on our summer vacations, we have to listen to the worst reproaches. How can you live in Germany! We tell them that we

Our Children Are at Home Here

have many friends and that Germans helped us establish ourselves, to begin anew.

But there are still too many of our generation whose parents suffered directly at the hands of the Germans. To them, to the children who never had any dealings with Nazis, who have lived in Israel all their lives, all Germans are Nazis. We've had some terrible arguments. One of my friends even went so far as to tell me to my face to imagine that the first man to sleep with my daughter will be a German. That's the very worst thing that can happen to a Jewish mother.

MICHAEL: Their reproaches are unfair, above all because we try to give our children here in Germany a Jewish education. We've found a small circle of Jews who are not so much concerned with the organized communal life as with the preservation of tradition and Jewish holidays.

ANNA: They all have children about the same age as ours.

MICHAEL: We celebrate the Jewish holidays together, and Anna has even begun to teach the children Hebrew. At first I wasn't sure whether this was a good idea or not, but now I'm all for it.

ANNA: Funny how things get reversed. In Israel the parents spoke Hebrew with us children and German with each other. Here Michael and I speak Hebrew with each other and German with our children. Our parents were also pleased that both of us came of German families. After all, it could have been a Pole or a Yemenite. But as it was, I brought them a *yecke*,* and that made them very happy. Michael's parents were pleased that they were able to speak German with me and with my parents. Neither of our parents was religious. My mother always said that after Hitler it was difficult to believe in God. God would not

* A somewhat derisive Israeli label for German Jews, derived from *jacket*, a reference to the Germans' greater formality of dress.

27

have permitted something like that to happen. And as to my father, I've never seen him set foot in a synagogue.

MICHAEL: But isn't it strange that we are going back to all that? We're all Jews, each in his own way. Now we celebrate the holidays; you are especially interested in that, Anna. My parents aren't religious either. Back in Germany they always had a Christmas tree. That's an absurd thing for a Jew.

ANNA: Right. My parents didn't have a tree when they lived in Europe. When I once asked my mother why not, she said, "Are you crazy? Jews with Christmas trees?" But my daughter, who is growing up here now, asks why we don't have a tree. All the other children have one, why don't we? In my mother's case it was different. Some children in her class were Jewish, and they didn't have Christmas trees either. I can't tell my daughter we don't celebrate Christmas and leave it at that. That's why we began again with the traditional celebrations. We observe Hanukkah. At Sukkoth we build a tabernacle and sit together around a table with honey and fruit telling stories. All of us, me included, love it. I didn't know any of this in my childhood. Today my daughter can say with much more self-assurance that we don't celebrate Christmas, but we have a real wild Hanukkah. Michael always says we don't need all this. . . .

MICHAEL: It's not as bad as all that. I just think it would be better for the children if they were totally integrated. It would be their best protection. It doesn't matter whether you're a Moslem or a Christian or a Jew. One shouldn't always stress the differences.

ANNA: But I'm not a German and don't want to be one. I still feel like an Israeli. Just as my parents never forgot the German language and didn't want to forget it, I cling to Hebrew and to my Israeli identity. Michael always tells me to get a German passport. It would make life simpler with things like visas when we travel. I might apply for one if it didn't mean that I'd have to relinquish the other one. But give up my Israeli passport? I couldn't do it.

MICHAEL: But somehow all this is overstated. After all, we're living here like anybody else. When I go into a shop to buy cheese nobody knows that I'm a Jew. I don't look like a stranger and don't talk like one. Why should I always emphasize the differences, why not what we have in common? You, too, are accepted here, or are you having problems?

ANNA: No, I'm doing all right. But don't forget, I'm well off now, but fifty years ago my parents were also doing well. No one would have believed then that within a few years the extermination of the Jews would begin. We can't make our past disappear. Why can't you see that? Whether we want to or not, the others see us as Jews.

MICHAEL: Now, don't exaggerate. Even then it took a few years. The gas chambers weren't built overnight. We would notice in time if it started again.

ANNA: I'll never forget something that happened when I first came to Germany, in 1967. I was attending a foreign-language school in Hamburg, the only student from Israel. A girl in the class came up to me and asked me whether I was Jewish. Then she asked me in astonishment how come I had such a small nose. Did I have it fixed? Didn't all Jews have big, hooked noses? I was shocked, absolutely speechless. My immediate reaction was that all those people at home were right, everybody here was a Nazi. I shared my room with a girl from Taiwan. She too was an unknown quantity. But at least they asked her questions about where she came from, what it was like, how they lived. Nobody asked me any questions, except for that stupid remark about my nose. The rest kept absolutely silent.

MICHAEL: But look at our daughters. They grew up here,

speak German like the Germans, have German friends, *are* Germans. Why turn them into Israelis now? Ever since they've been studying Hebrew they go around proudly telling everybody that they are Germans and Israelis. I'm not so sure that that's a good thing.

They are ten and seven, respectively. Perhaps they'll always live here. They are lucky in that they have very liberal teachers. But things could be different. True, we are living very peacefully and without any major problems. But the Germans haven't gotten over the trauma of World War II. I notice it also with the men I work with. The strict way they bring up their children, that constant pursuit of discipline and order.

ANNA: But we have our friends. They are entirely different. There are also many other Germans who are not at all like that.

MICHAEL: Who's talking about our friends? People of our age, blue-collar workers, auto mechanics, laborers, I see them every day. Then there are those with the starched collars, around the age of fifty. They say, forget about all that old shit, who still wants to know anything about the Nazis, it's been over for a long time. All of them were in the Hitler Youth and talk about what a tough time they had as children. Guilt? Crimes? That's not for them. And the young people? They scare me the most. They know nothing. They glorify the past and look for some radicalization, maybe because they're so bored.

ANNA: Do you think it's any different in Israel? I was riding in a bus in Tel Aviv last year when a girl standing in front of me, maybe twelve years old, threw a falafel out the window. I thought to myself, what, here in Israel? Can't be. I walked up to her and asked whether she couldn't wait until she got off, that one doesn't do things like that. You should have heard how she dusted me off. "Is it your street or your falafel?" she yelled at me. "Leave me alone, mind your own business."

Our Children Are at Home Here

What kind of culture is that? Do you think a generation of good people has sprung up there? No, they're just as snotty there, and that hurts me. I was always so proud of our land, of the blooming desert, of every tree and bush that grew there. But now I'm disillusioned. As far as politics is concerned, I'm dismayed by what is happening in Israel today. What have we learned from our past? When I travel through Germany, through Schleswig-Holstein or the Black Forest, everything is beautiful. But for me that countryside lacks the feeling, the memories, the scents, the sense of belonging. Have you ever smelled orange blossoms here, even in the loveliest landscape? At this time of year all of Israel smells of them. You breathe in and you're intoxicated.

MICHAEL: I feel the same. Remember when we went to see that Israeli movie recently? The plot didn't matter. But to begin with, it was in Hebrew, and then it was shot in places we knew. We kept on nudging each other, remembering that we'd stood here, that there was a restaurant we knew, a street, and so on. It was like being back home for two hours.

ANNA: And still, all that is only a romantic dream. In two years you'll be forty, the children are growing up, and one day they'll say, "You want to go to Israel? All right, but we're staying here." Leave our children? They are the only thing we have. The longer we stay here, the harder it will be to leave and go back.

MICHAEL: When we came to Berlin, your mother advised us to contact the Community. A short, stocky man greeted us and asked us all sorts of questions. Then suddenly he began to speak Hebrew and said that he had to ask a very intimate question. We were startled. We were married, had been married by a rabbi. What he asked us was: "Why did you leave? What are you doing here?" I was furious and thought to myself, you old

31

Zionist, you've been sitting here in Germany for the last thirty years and playing at being a supporter of Israel. But I controlled myself. After all, there was that apartment I wanted. So I told him that we were planning to stay only for a short time and that of course we were going back.

ANNA: That's what also bothered me the most about the Community. That constant talk about returning, particularly when they talk to the young. They keep their children here, send a check to Israel every year as a sop to their conscience, and fight with our blood. They know only too well that when we return Michael must go into the army right away. We're supposed to risk our necks so that back here they can enjoy their sense of security in the form of Israel.

When Israel marched into Lebanon, we signed an appeal protesting the Lebanon campaign, whereupon we were promptly looked on as PLO agents. We were hounded, just like in an anti-Communist propaganda campaign. But we have found our type of Jews, ours, not those organized in the Community.

When my father was received by Kreisky in Austria, he sat there and thought to himself, See, we're sitting here, two Jews driven out of Vienna. One of them sits under the portrait of the emperor and pays homage to the one sitting across the table. Neither is religious, neither goes to the synagogue, neither belongs to the Community. Yet both survived the Holocaust by chance and have again made their way to the top.

MICHAEL: Your father doesn't even consider himself a war victim. When we told him that a book about the children of survivors was in the works, he said quite spontaneously, "How come? I'm not a survivor, I wasn't in a concentration camp." Apparently we Jews think that having to flee, being driven out, is nothing extraordinary. As long as they let us live, being driven

Our Children Are at Home Here

out is quite normal. And every pogrom makes us more restless. Every place becomes a hotel where we come for a brief stay, already thinking about moving on to the next place. We may not yet know where we're going, but we suspect that we'll have to leave again, regardless of how well we like it where we are.

But we are still lucky with these fantasies. The story of your uncle's wife shows us that in the past some fared far worse.

ANNA: Yes, she's living in Prague. Her husband and her daughter were killed in Auschwitz. For years she went to train stations, day after day, to wait for them. And when my father visited her, she set the table for four. During the meal she constantly spoke to her husband and her daughter, both long dead.

And when we left Israel, my father said to me, "You are going to a country where they speak the language of Herzl and Hitler. . . ."

3

Jeanette

My Home Is Inside Myself

Y LIFE is like a novel, a bad novel, but I haven't given up hope. On the contrary. I can now speak about the past full of hope for the future. But the past will always color everything I do.

Even telling about my birth is a problem. I don't know anything precise. My grandmother and my mother told me different versions. I know that I was born in Berlin at the end of December 1945. My mother was seventeen and still going to school. She'd spent the war years in Berlin. I don't know how she survived here. At any rate, her mother had had her baptized before the war. Her father was dead. I was twelve before I found out who my father was, but even that story might be a fiction. At about that age I started getting after my mother to tell me about my father, most of all where he was. She told me, reluctantly, that he was a Russian soldier, a Jew from Kiev, a teacher by profession. She said that she had known him only briefly and that he disappeared before I was born. He had given her his name and his address in Kiev, but he never answered any of the letters she wrote him. She never heard from him again.

So that's my father, a Jewish phantom. There is no picture of him, no letter, nothing that could remind me of him, except that my grandmother said that I resembled him. So I was born at the end of December at the Berlin Charité hospital, a premature baby, maybe the first occupation baby, the child of a baptized half-Jewish mother and a Jewish Red Army soldier father, neither of whom wanted any part of me.

Nine months after I was born my mother disappeared and left me with my grandmother. From then on I called my grandmother "Mommy" and my mother "Mama," but both were only poor substitutes for what I wanted, something I continue to long for. All of a sudden I had nobody. The grandmother became the mother, the mother was gone, the father was never mentioned, the grandfather was long dead. I was living in an emotional vacuum. Talking about my father was taboo, and even as a child at school, when I was asked about him I would say that I had no father. And I didn't know what to make of the frequently cynical remarks I heard that somewhere there was sure to be one.

So I grew up at my grandmother's in East Berlin, and she really loved me, even if her love consisted mainly of prohibitions. She forced me into a Jewish tradition that meant nothing to me. She was strict, embittered, and often also unfair. Probably it was too much for her, bringing up a child alone at her age. But my first Jewish experiences were gained through her. She dragged me to synagogue, told me about Jewish feast days, about kosher food, but always without any real feeling. They were stories of a lost world, fairy tales that were alien to me and that I listened to without any awareness that they had something to do with me. It never occurred to me, despite all my grandmother's efforts, that I myself might be Jewish.

But the lies about my father turned into an insurmountable problem. I began to tell the other children stories that I had seen him but that he'd had to hide, and God knows what else.

Then, when I was eleven, my grandmother became very ill. She went to the hospital and I to a children's home. She wasn't expected to recover, so finding a home for me became a problem. It was a terrible time. I remember being dragged from one foster home to another for inspection. I was supposed to help in the decision. But my grandmother recovered and came home, and I returned to her. Yet the fear of having to go to a home if she should die became so great that I felt I absolutely had to leave. At that time my mother was living in West Germany. I tried every way I could to join her. I spoke of it constantly, said that I'd take off, that I would never stay in a home, and I didn't let up until I was sent to her.

What happened then was a nightmare. My mother could do nothing with me. She beat me, made me do all the housework, and treated me like a maid. I went back to my grandmother in East Berlin, but again I began to be afraid of having to go to a home, and so I was left to decide between a mother to whom I was a burden and a grandmother who was old and ill and couldn't keep me much longer. Again I fled. At age eleven I got on a train in West Berlin, without a ticket, and went to Hamburg. There I changed trains, but I was taken off by the railway police. They notified my mother and she came for me.

That's when I began to get interested in my father and wouldn't stop asking questions until my mother told me the story about the Jewish soldier from Kiev. Suddenly a lot of things began to make sense. My father was a Jew. That explained my grandmother's forays into Judaism, my feeling of being an out-

My Home Is Inside Myself

sider, my different looks, my being treated differently, the questions people asked about whether I was Jewish—everything suddenly fit together like a jigsaw puzzle in which the individual pieces at first make no sense. That's when for the first time, all by myself, I went into town to attend services at a synagogue. And they took me in as though they'd been waiting for me all my life. Suddenly I was surrounded by warmth and affection. I received religious instruction from the cantor, and I had found a home. At the time I looked very Jewish, with my thick black hair and prominent nose. I thought I was ugly. All these blonde girls in my class had friends, were popular. Only I looked different and talked different. But here in the synagogue everybody looked like me. I first noticed this when my teacher asked me whether I would give German lessons to two girls from South America. One look at them and I saw how much they resembled me. When I found out that they had in fact come from South America via Israel, it became more and more clear to me why I was so different.

The synagogue in the city where I lived with my mother was like a small family. Only a few Jews were living there at the time, and the holiday services ended with communal meals. There was laughter and singing and I felt they all loved me.

But I also became Jewish in my dealings with Germans, and they must have felt it. When I was still living with my grandmother, people would take me for French or Italian. Now I was seen as Jewish. Complete strangers on the street or in shops would come up to me to tell me that they'd had Jewish friends and hadn't known anything about the persecutions. In school I became the token Jew. Whenever anything having to do with Jews came up, the teacher would turn to me obsequiously and ask, "Isn't that right, Jeanette?" Her helpfulness and fawning was so offensive that I became suspicious. When she promoted me even though I'd done poor work, I began to be curious about her motives. I found out by chance that under the Nazis some teachers had been arrested after she had denounced them, and that she had also made life hell for the Jews and Communists in her class. I found her special treatment of me so offensive that I couldn't function. First, my schoolwork suffered, and then I developed psychosomatic illnesses, circulatory disorders that started me on an Odyssey through hospitals and doctors' offices, but nobody could help me. According to one opinion, my heart was too small but that it would grow, and I was sent to Helgoland for a cure. After six weeks there I looked for a job. I was done with school, and also with the synagogue and my contact with other Jews. I stayed in Helgoland for a year, taking any work I could get—chambermaid, shopgirl, waitress. I was away from my mother, was earning my own living, and felt good about being on my own for the first time and having at least a small degree of independence.

But I didn't want to be a chambermaid for the rest of my life. After that year I was eager for an education. I wanted to show the world what I could do, so I decided to go to Berlin and finish high school.

In the meantime my grandmother had moved to West Berlin. She had aged, but she was feeling better and I went to live with her.

Times were hard for me then. I took any job, no matter what, to earn money so I could go to school. All my grandmother had was a tiny pension, and I certainly couldn't expect any money from my mother.

I finished high school and began to study psychology. That is also when I met my husband. He wasn't a Jew, but he knew more about Judaism and Jewish history than I did. He was

My Home Is Inside Myself

incredibly well informed in this field. I sometimes think that I was a living object of his studies.

We married in 1968 and became completely immersed in the student movement. Of course we lived in a commune, joined every demonstration, had discussions that went on all night; I felt that I was part of a large movement. I took on a new identity, full of illusions of finally having found a new home, a home of real people, of friends, comrades, and fellow activists. When my husband and I moved into our own apartment, I wanted to forget my Jewish past. In Berlin I had no contact with other Jews or with the Community. The Jewish me no longer existed. All of us moved close together; the warmth came from the movement, from the bond created by the common enemy, and from the illusion of finally being one among many.

And to remove the last vestige of being different, I did something I regret to this day. I had my nose fixed. I had it cut off, my Jewish nose, had it trimmed down to an ordinary German nose. This dream of finally being no different from the others made me forget everything that made up my past and my identity. For years I felt guilty about that damned nose job. I accused myself of having betrayed my Jewishness, most of all because those illusions about a new community and sense of belonging turned out to be a pipe dream.

My daughter was born in 1969, after which my marriage unfortunately went to pieces. I had to interrupt my studies and now lived alone with my daughter. Once again everything was in ruins. The commune had broken up, I had a child without a father, and too little money to both study and take care of my child and myself. The student movement was anything but a home, and I'd had the Jewish part of myself removed surgically.

When my daughter was about two I was invited to a

Christmas party by friends of mine. I wasn't particularly interested in the whole business. I sat in a corner of the room near the
Christmas tree and watched my daughter. She was sitting under
the decorated tree with its candles and sweets, playing with a gift
she had gotten. I was astonished how indifferent and bored she
was by the tree. No shining eyes, no blissful expression, no
astonishment over the burning candles and silver angels, nothing. She played the same way she always did at home.

At that point I thought to myself, this can't go on. You have a
daughter growing up in a total vacuum, without tradition and
identity. She is not Jewish, and she will never be a real German.
Christmas doesn't interest her and she doesn't know a thing
about Hanukkah.

I decided to rejoin the Jews. But this time it wasn't so easy.
Here in Berlin they ask for proof. I didn't have any. I returned to
the city my mother lived in and found out that I had never been
officially accepted into the Jewish Community there. They did
not give me the papers I needed for the Community in Berlin. I
was Nobody—neither Jew nor Christian, and a German only on
paper. Was I maybe a Russian?

I still had the name and address of my father, and so I went to
Kiev on a tour and found the street and building, but nobody
there knew him. I talked to people who'd lived there for more
than thirty years. Not one of them knew a Jew, a teacher, who
was supposed to have lived there and been a soldier in Germany.
The father remained an illusion, and all I knew of him was that,
according to my mother, he was forever fiddling around with his
motorbike. That's all she could tell me about him. Later, at the
hotel, I found out that the street I had gone to was one of Kiev's
main streets and the name he had given was as common as
Smith or Jones. What would a Berliner in Kiev say if asked for
his name and address and he didn't want to tell the truth? He'd

probably come up with just such a common name and well-known street. It was hopeless. I gave up.

Back in Berlin I was determined to become a member of the Jewish Community. It was the only home left to me. At the conversion ceremony, when I stood in front of the rabbi, he looked at me and asked, "Why do you want to convert? You're already Jewish." It felt good to hear him say this, even if it was a type of racism, this classification based on looks. But I was glad. I was accepted into the Community.

I had already been sending my daughter to the Jewish kindergarten for some time and wanted to bring her up as a Jew. We went to synagogue regularly and I tried to instill in her an interest in and understanding of Judaism. Now she is becoming more independent, a little resistant, and she no longer accepts everything automatically. Still I hope and believe that she will always think of herself as Jewish.

I didn't finish my studies. Instead I became a librarian, not an ideal substitute, but at least it's a profession. I have a job that allows me to support my daughter and myself, we have a nice apartment, and I do have relationships, unfortunately no lasting ones. I find being alone more difficult than I had thought. But I have found friends, good friends. The return to Judaism, to Jewish friends, was a return to a home I had deserted. And I even have enough self-confidence to feel good about my role as an outsider. Not being like most of the others and still not being lonely is a pleasant combination of feelings, and I am beginning to appreciate it.

There's also a group of Jews here who are not very involved in the Community. Most of them are left-wing, active in politics or the arts, and they meet regularly. This group helps stiffen the spine, give us moral support and courage. It is good to know that they exist, that in addition to those who have children, who celebrate the feast days, there are others we can call on, to know that we are not alone and not outsiders.

For there is one thing I have learned in these unquiet days of my life: the home for which I had been searching so desperately can be found only inside myself.

4

Tuvi

We Can Also Defend Ourselves

I'M a policeman. When I went to pick up my two children at my mother's house a few days ago, I took off my jacket in the foyer before going into the living room. Only my mother's frightened, nervous expression reminded me that I'd forgotten something. Quickly, before she could begin to scream, I went back and took off my gun and holster. She doesn't want to see me with a weapon. It's hard enough for her to understand that her son, a Jew, is in the German police. She's never criticized me for it, but before I joined both my parents asked me to think it over carefully. But my mother often shouts, when she sees me in my uniform, "Don't carry yourself like that! Don't stand like that!" And most of all she doesn't want to see the pistol. It must remind her of all sorts of terrible things. I don't know what it is, she never talks about it, but I can see it in her face, her eyes, her nervous screaming. She spent the entire war here in Germany. Her mother was a Christian who converted to Judaism when she married my grandfather but then reconverted to Christianity when the Nazis came. My mother survived here in Germany as a half-Jew, which is more than a miracle. For example, she couldn't go to a shelter during air raids but had to wait in the open air until the all-clear. She never talks about that time, but I have a good enough imagination to understand why she becomes so tense and excited when she sees me in my uniform. Her nerves are shot. Her Christian relatives were very helpful to her during that time, or she would never have survived. They also existed, those other Germans.

After the war she went to Israel, where she met my father. He was born in Vienna and spent the war years in Israel. He came on one of those ships that brought illegal immigrants. It was attacked while lying in the harbor, and it sank. Actually the Jewish underground fighters in Palestine just wanted to disable the ship to prevent the British from sending it back again, but they damaged it so badly that it sank. It was the *Patrias*. Everybody knows the story. Almost a thousand people were aboard, and about seven hundred drowned. My father managed to save himself even though he couldn't swim. He once told me that he was lucky and was able to get out of his cabin by climbing through a porthole, and the English then rescued him. But apart from that I know almost nothing about my parents. Especially my father wraps himself in silence. His family wasn't able to escape and all perished. When the subject comes up—my wife sometimes asks him, I can't—one can see his face change. He always says, "You can ask me anything you like." But then instead of an answer there are tears. Only a year ago I found out by chance that he'd had a sister. I don't even know what his father did. But how can I ask him when it still upsets him so much after all these years?

I was born in Israel and came to Germany when I was six. I

We Can Also Defend Ourselves

have happy memories of those early years. We lived in Haifa, near the sea, and the beach was my playground. It was always warm, we were always outdoors, always dirty, and no one minded. One of my first experiences after coming to Germany was when a furious woman with an umbrella chased me off the grass in the park. That was a shock, and also quite crazy. Suddenly everything was orderly, the people were grumpy, and children anyway didn't matter. But I got used to everything, went to school here like all the others, and never had any problems about my Jewishness.

For my parents things were much harder. They came to Germany without any money, without work, and without a place to live. The Germans had long since gotten back on their feet. The economic miracle was in full swing, they again had things, they again were somebody. My parents came too late to profit from the recovery.

Then, with the help of the Jewish Community, my father found a job in the laundry of the Jewish hospital. The Community also helped them find an apartment. Later a rich uncle—thank God there's one in every family—also helped, and my parents were able to open their own laundry. But it took years before they could pay off all their debts.

Despite all the difficulties, my parents were glad to be back in Germany. My mother's parents, who also had gone to Israel after the war, had returned before her. They never felt at home in Israel. The climate, the Oriental way of life, the language, everything was strange to them. They were real Germans, *yeckes*. Like many other relatives of my mother they'd been Germans before Hitler and remained Germans despite Hitler. They actually were glad to come back. And many others who weren't able to come back feel sorry for themselves, like my friend Moshe, for example. When he's in Israel he rushes around, is nervous and excited, criticizes everything, but he lives there. When he comes here he is happy, relaxed, and free. He wanted to come to Germany, but then he divorced his wife and married a Yemenite. Now his ex-wife is here in Germany and he's in Israel, because his second wife doesn't want to come here. So there he sits in Israel and gripes.

I was brought up to have a Jewish consciousness. It was taken for granted that I would go to the Jewish kindergarten and later to the Jewish youth group. My Jewishness was a part of me from early childhood on. And in school I was never bothered or teased because of it. Of course I got into lots of fights, but never because I was Jewish. Everyone knew what I was; there were no secrets. That was always my way. I don't believe in hiding or in secrets. On the contrary. I had a friend in school, also Jewish, who had a much harder time. He came from an Orthodox family and so was brought up much stricter than I. My parents were much more liberal. We rode on Saturday, and I ate pizzas even though they aren't kosher. But he obeyed all the rules. He also didn't go to school on Saturday. But they had an automatic timer on their TV, which turned on the sports broadcasts on Saturday. That was okay, as long as they didn't turn it on themselves. I guess everyone has a right to practice his Judaism as he sees fit.

But the following strange thing happened. As I said, this fellow had been brought up very Jewish. You'd think that he would have a highly developed Jewish consciousness. Not so. He always wanted to hide his Jewishness, keep it secret. When he was with Christians, he never talked about it and acted as though he were ashamed of his background. When you said anything to him about it he became upset, as though he had been caught doing something forbidden. I was the one who flaunted my Jewishness, but he was the one who ran into prob-

We Can Also Defend Ourselves

lems. He was bullied and had some bad run-ins, while I was always accepted as a Jew. Perhaps it depends on how you deal with others. We Jews, especially here in Germany, must learn not to put up with everything. We must show the others that we've learned to defend ourselves. Just like in Israel today. I may not agree with a lot that's going on there, but I'm impressed that there now are Jews who stand up and say: "Never again!"

I think that when I was a boy this attitude worked to my advantage. The teachers always treated me with kid gloves, as though they were afraid of doing something wrong, something that might be held against them.

I was also the kind who would keep relatively calm for a long time but then suddenly explode. And when that happened, there was no holding me back. I can remember one time when I almost killed someone at my school. It was in grade school; I was still very small and carried my books in a backpack. The others all had real briefcases, but my parents had come to Germany only a short time before and were quite poor compared with the others and couldn't afford such a briefcase. They had to start from scratch, while all those good Germans who had survived Hitler were once again stinking rich. At any rate, one of those types kept on ribbing me because of my book bag. One day he grabbed me from behind; I let go of the backpack straps and he fell down. I pounced on him and grabbed him by the throat. If a policeman hadn't come by just then I might have killed him. From that day on nobody ever bothered me again. Although I was small and delicate they were afraid of me, and that was fine with me.

Aside from that episode, I have very positive memories of my schooldays. I was often asked about Jewish practices—why we don't celebrate Christmas or why some men cover their heads. It made me proud to tell them about all these things. And later, as I got older, I felt that a new generation of Germans was growing up, a generation different than those who'd chased my parents out.

I also had some weird experiences. One of them sounds like a movie. As a teenager I often went on trips with the youth group of the Jewish Community. It was like the Boy Scouts, with campfires and cookouts. Once—I won't forget this as long as I live—we were sitting around the fire, singing our songs, when a fellow about seventeen years old came over to us and asked whether he could join us. He was wearing some sort of uniform. It turned out that he was part of a neo-Nazi group that was holding military exercises nearby. At first he didn't know that we were Jews. When it dawned on him, his face became rigid and he wanted to jump up and leave. But we asked him all sorts of questions and didn't let him leave right away. It turned out that his father had been an SS officer and that both his parents were still enthusiastic Nazis who hated Jews and dreamed of a new Hitler. Somehow we managed to keep him from leaving right away. He stayed for quite a while and we talked. When he left we invited him to our youth center. We didn't really think that we'd ever see him again, but a few days later there he was. He began to come more and more often, and he became interested in Judaism. A little later he went to the rabbi for instruction, converted to Judaism, and emigrated to Israel. There he volunteered for the army and became an Israeli citizen. In the October War he served as a parachutist in the Israeli army. He was critically wounded and is still on the disabled list. A former Nazi sacrificed himself for the Jews. The parents are miserable and their son is disabled—the twists and turns of fate.

Nobody knows this story. It hasn't appeared in any newspaper, and nobody pays attention to such heroes. But for me stories like this are important, especially here in Germany. I can't keep

We Can Also Defend Ourselves

on saying, like the other Jews here, that nothing has changed and that the Germans are still swine. The people here have also been changed by the war, and today we are living here in one of the world's greatest democracies.

Unfortunately I didn't finish high school, something I regret to this day. I went into the hotel business. That's when I also started to get involved with girls. My mother began to get after me not to marry a Christian. I had a few affairs with Christian girls, but things really began to get ticklish when I got involved with Jewish girls. In this small Jewish Community everybody knows immediately who goes with whom and when and where. And then the parents get into the act, wanting to know what's going on, whether we plan to marry, and so on. You feel beleaguered until you yourself decide that you want to get married. I did marry a Jewish girl. It was a big wedding, with three hundred guests, a huge affair. But after that, when we were alone together, there was nothing. Everything was just an illusion, a fulfillment of other people's wishes. We didn't understand each other, weren't really a pair, and after a few weeks we separated. She wanted to go to Israel and I didn't. I had meanwhile become the assistant manager of a hotel and didn't want to leave. But because of all this pressure and the disappointment of our marriage, I was the one who from one day to the next quit my job and went to Israel. It was the first time since leaving in 1960— eighteen years before—that I had been in Israel. I worked on a kibbutz, and actually it was a nice time. But I had some violent arguments with Jews from other countries. When they found out that I came from Germany they really went after me. I was constantly asked how it was possible for a Jew to live in Germany after all that had happened. But most of them had no idea, had never been here, had no experience with Germany, not during the war and certainly not afterward.

TUVI

They said that anyone living in Germany today was a traitor, was betraying the dead. That used to really upset me. Here were people coming from the worst totalitarian countries like Chile, Argentina, and Russia trying to tell me about democracy and freedom. And when they asked me how I could live in Germany after all that had happened, I asked them how they could live in countries in which hundreds of thousands simply disappeared every year, where people were being tortured and murdered, not in the time of Hitler but now, when human rights are being talked about everywhere.

But nothing I said made any difference. For them, Germany remained a criminal state, and one simply shouldn't live there. I certainly don't want to minimize what happened here under the Nazis. But these unbelievable, fiendish crimes have been made out to be even more fiendish, if that is possible. And this hatred of Germany and everything German has been handed on to the children. They drink it down like mother's milk. They come from all over the world, without having experienced the persecution in Germany, many of them not even having lost any relatives, and they sit around and make money and tell me what a horror it is to live as a Jew in Germany.

I'd rather live here than in some South American dictatorship or under so-called socialism or in a country like the Spain of recent memory. Even countries like Belgium and Sweden are, I think, far more conservative than Germany.

Still, at the time I wanted to stay in Israel. I met my present wife there and returned to Germany only to get a divorce. But then I stayed here and had my wife follow me. For a time I was unemployed, and then I applied to the police. I'm now working as an ordinary patrolman. I wear the uniform and obey the rules. Just like before at the hotel. There I also wore a uniform and obeyed rules.

We Can Also Defend Ourselves

At first my wife was shocked when I told her I wanted to join the police. But I told her about all the advantages, and she was persuaded. If we had stayed in Israel, I would have had to serve in the military and would have been involved in the whole Lebanon business. When I think of that I prefer the police force here in Germany.

At the time I thought about it all very soberly and without emotion. A neighbor of my parents is a police officer, and I consulted with him. The most important point for me is the possibility of finishing high school and perhaps even getting a higher education. At any other job I would have to do it at night.

Of course, I had some unpleasant experiences, especially during the training period. But just like my early school years, I let the others know where I drew the line. At first there were some who would begin to tell Jewish jokes, and when this threatened to get out of hand I went up to them and said, "Okay, you've had your fun, but now lay off."

And that was that. That's all I had to do. A firm word and they pulled back.

Of course one can't react hysterically to everything. When they were drunk, someone might start singing the Horst Wessel song. But I don't necessarily see this as a conscious anti-Semitic provocation. They're not Nazis, just drunks who don't know what they're doing. It's a kind of tradition, combined with the way they were brought up. Of course there are anti-foreigners and anti-Semites in the police, but no more and no less than among the rest of the German population.

I've always been treated with fairness, even with special consideration, by my superiors. I was a little older than most, and so they often went easy on me. I never took part in all that nonsense about military tactics, taking cover, and so on, and nobody said anything.

The people in the police today are different from fifteen or twenty years ago. The old army officers and Nazi policemen are gone. We now have a liberal police force that has nothing more to do with the Hitler era. Perhaps I'm only being self-serving, but I am convinced that those types are a thing of the past. An end has been written to that era. Of course for a time after the war the same people who had arrested the Jews were in the police. But that's over and done with. When I began my training, I decided that I would leave immediately if anything out of line happened. I would have thrown the uniform into the garbage can, because I won't take any nonsense. But nothing happened. On the contrary, everybody was friendly and helpful. After a few months I was even proudly shown off as one of their best.

Today I am no longer afraid in Germany. I'm more afraid of the atom bomb than of any possible persecution. But I also don't have any patriotic feeling for the country. I don't care whether a German soccer team wins or how many Olympic medals the Germans get. I am more interested in how Israel is doing.

But I have confidence in this country. True, some neo-Nazis have tried to gain a foothold again, but they haven't gotten very far. And the extreme Left hasn't either. Neither has won popular support. If that weren't so—and I am watching what goes on here very carefully—I would leave immediately and not spend another day here. I am not ashamed to say this, despite my sympathy for Germany. Perhaps I wouldn't leave immediately but instead try to organize some sort of resistance.

I like to get involved in what I believe in. But I have two children and a wife, and I wouldn't sacrifice them, so I'd try to escape in time.

My brother had an experience that proved to me that people can defend themselves if they stick together. He once went on a

We Can Also Defend Ourselves

skiing trip to the mountains with a group of Jews, I think to some place in Bavaria. They stopped at an inn for a meal. Sitting at the next table was a young local farmer wearing a leather armband with a swastika and a slogan, something like "Jews get out." One of the group turned to him and asked him what the armband was supposed to mean. He answered that everything, unemployment and the economic crisis, was the fault of the Jews. My brother then asked him whether he knew what Jews looked like. Of course, he said, they were short, weak, had black hair and long noses, and they stank. When one of the others told him that he was a Jew and asked him what he thought of that, the farmer yelled at him that he was an asshole like all the others and should have been gassed along with them. One word led to another, there was a lot of shouting, more people came from the village, and before long they were all outside and fighting. The upshot was that nobody in the village dared bother them again. Things calmed down and stayed that way. They slapped them down and they became quiet. That's one way of handling things.

I had an experience that was almost the opposite of my brother's. As a teenager I went to Holland with the Community. We were a group of young Jews, all about the same age, and we were made to feel extremely unwelcome by the people of the town where we stayed in a youth hostel. It went so far that often we were not even waited on when we went shopping. But then the people found out that we were German Jews. From that moment on everything changed. The people became so friendly it was almost embarrassing. A play was put on for us, we were invited by the mayor and were given gifts. The people knocked themselves out for us. It was a unique experience. We were not only German Jews, but Germans and Jews. They hated the one part of us and had compassion for the other. There was no balance here. Without transition going from aversion to sympathy and the other way round—that seems to be the fate of the German Jews.

But the decision whether to be a Jew or German is one that all of us living in Germany have to make. I know of no German Jews in whom the two identities blend. Even I, who have so much sympathy for this new Germany, have no clear-cut answer to this question. First comes the Jew and then the German, if one can be a German at all. If it's possible at all, then perhaps one could be a Jew who lives in Germany and holds a German passport.

For me the absurdity of the division between German and Jew is revealed on the soccer field. No Jews play on the soccer team of the Jewish sports club. We're only substitutes. Because German law bars discrimination in sports, more and more non-Jews who are good players have joined us.

Now these poor Germans, the kind of pure Aryans the Nazis would have loved, run around on the soccer field wearing the uniforms of the Jewish club and are heckled by some of the people in the stands. There is the usual name-calling and slogans, "Out with the Jews," and "Into the gas," and lots more. And our poor Aryans lose their cool when that happens. Some have been known to charge into the stands and attack the hecklers.

Can you think of a more grotesque twist to the problem of anti-Semitism than this?

5

Susan

I Couldn't Have Survived

LATELY I've come to realize how much I resemble my parents. Both of them were able to escape the Nazis in time and come to New York. They have described their life in America and the first years of emigration often and in great detail, but never a word about their childhood in Germany, the years before their departure. And the murder of their relatives, the experiences of those who survived the camps, is never mentioned. And what about me, forty years later? I am thirty-six and have a six-year-old daughter. I keep on thinking that I ought to tell her about her ancestors. But I can't. I simply can't say to her, "You are a German Jew and live in a country in which forty years ago almost all Jews were gassed or otherwise murdered."

What I would be telling her about aren't even my personal experiences. It would only be a description, a story. But it would sound so simple, so banal, that single, brutal sentence, like something out of a fairy tale with evil witches and sorcerers. There is also something ludicrous about it when it is stated so flatly. What happened at that time is not fit to be told.

Above all I now understand my father's silence a little better. My mother would occasionally tell some anecdotes about the time before the war. The little I know of this period in my father's life I learned from my mother. Perhaps the reason is that most of my mother's family were able to save themselves, while most of my father's perished.

I can remember a situation at home that bothered me for years. Actually it still does. We'd be sitting in the living room and someone would get the idea of looking at old pictures. Boxes of snapshots and old photo albums would be dragged out. But the oldest pictures went back only to the time when my parents were already in the United States. There were almost none from their childhood, except for one of my father and his brother as children, standing in front of a couple, and also a girl. Every time this picture was shown, then or later, my father said that the one child was his brother and the other one he himself. Nobody asked who the other people in the picture were. I was always fairly certain that the couple were my father's parents, who were murdered in Auschwitz, and that the girl might be a sister who also was murdered. A couple of years ago I finally got up the courage to ask my mother. I could never have asked my father about it. She told me that the girl was a friend and that she, too, was dead. She didn't tell me her name. The grandparents' names also were never mentioned. And I never got up enough nerve to ask.

My father came from a small village in Germany. His father was a cattle dealer. The entire family was completely nonpolitical. I know almost more about his brother, who was a rather aggressive child, than about him. When the first anti-Semitic excesses began and somebody on the street would taunt him and

I Couldn't Have Survived

call him a dirty Jew, he'd fight. His parents therefore sent him away early on, in the beginning of the thirties, to a yeshiva in Poland. From there he wanted to go to America, but he got stuck in Shanghai when the war broke out. I don't know when and how my father got to New York, but I know how he found his brother again, and it's a wild story. After the war his brother met an American soldier in a synagogue in Shanghai. He told him that he thought that his brother was in New York. The soldier said that he, too, came from New York and asked his name. It turned out that the soldier was a friend of my father's, and so the two sole survivors of the family were reunited. My uncle now lives in New York and is a Hasidic rabbi.

My mother talks much more about her past. She too had lived in a small village in Germany before the war, and her father too was a cattle dealer.

In 1933 she was only ten years old, but before she was able to leave in 1939 she went through some terrible times. The entire village terrorized her family, and she would often be beaten up by the other children. Only rarely does she go into any more detail. But one story I remember. She and her sister were sick in bed with the measles. Suddenly a howling mob appeared, threw stones at their window, shouting, "Jewish pigs," and the like.

Another story, this one told by my father, is very curious. He was always a good athlete, but as the discrimination increased, he was excluded from all sports. But he was such a good soccer player that the Hitler Youth got him into their games. Maybe his playmates were the same ones who some years later came for his parents and loaded them on the cattle car. I don't know, but for me today it is all simply unimaginable. I miss knowing about the everyday incidents of that time. You always hear about the major catastrophes: escape or death, survival or extermination. Everything is so vague and fantastic. Except for a few anecdotes everything is eradicated. Once in the mid-seventies I visited my father's village with him, and it was very unpleasant and almost eerie for me. We were standing in the village square when an old man came up to us. He recognized my father, smiled at him, and said, "Well, we always said that the Jew Goldstein was the smartest one in the class."

He said it without blushing, as though nothing had happened between then and now. No guilt feeling, no apology, nothing. But my father also was friendly. I found the situation intolerable. But my father doesn't know hatred. I think he simply wants to forget, wants to have peace at last.

A few years ago we were all sitting in front of the TV watching a film about the time of the Nazis. When the scenes about Kristallnacht came on, my father fell asleep. He sat there and snored, missing this gruesome part of his own past. Today my parents like to spend their vacation in Austria. German is spoken there, and yet it isn't Germany. Everything is so neat and clean, the landscape so beautiful. I think it reminds them of the good times of their childhood.

In New York they live in a real ghetto. Only German-speaking Jews. When I was born, in 1947, it must have seemed like a miracle. I was one of the first postwar children in my parents' circle. After all those years in which death was a daily occurrence, the creation of this new life was something very special.

At first I was supposed to become a real American. My parents spoke only English with me, but German with each other. We lived in a neighborhood that was half Irish and half Jewish. Here I experienced anti-Semitism for the first time. Once, on my way to school, I bumped into two Irish girls. The minute they saw me they spat and called me Christ-killer. I was scared but also so angry that I got into a fight with them. But otherwise my childhood was untroubled. I had a religious upbringing; we

I Couldn't Have Survived

celebrated all the holidays and lit Sabbath candles. My parents also were involved in temple activities, but I think they became religious only after leaving Germany.

In 1939 they came out of Hell into Paradise. The snapshots of their early years in New York are mostly group pictures with many happy, smiling faces. They also say that to them it seemed like a miracle to be allowed to work in a shop, to go to a beach on weekends or to a movie in the evening. They still feel very indebted to the United States. They were shocked by my increasingly critical attitude toward the government. They simply couldn't understand it. America had saved their lives, and therefore it was a good country. Every demonstration, even one against the war and for peace, reminded them of the Nazis, of strutting Storm Troopers, of destruction and death. All they wanted was to be left in peace. And they never had any desire to return to Germany. They own a small business in New York and feel comfortable there.

For me Germany was something utterly alien. There was no past; America represented the future. Almost all my parents' friends were emigrants, but most of them had come to New York in their youth. Hardly any of them had been to a concentration camp. As a child I never felt as though I belonged to a minority. Of the thirty-eight children in my class, only three were not Jewish. Germany was far away, the Nazis were long gone, and I was concerned with more important matters than the history of the Jews in Germany.

Only when I went to college and left my small town in the big city did I experience things which hinted that I was somewhat alien or different. I once took a course at an out-of-state college. The first day I noticed that except for one other girl, who also was Jewish, all the other students were tall, blue-eyed, and blond. She and I were assigned the same dormitory room. This was the first time I experienced the same sense of loneliness I was later to feel in Germany, this painful awareness of how few of us there are, and moreover that there is no feeling of community among those few.

After finishing college I taught school and began to travel in Europe. I went everywhere—Scandinavia, England, Spain, France, Italy. Germany was the only country I avoided. I didn't want to see it even though I was very curious about the villages my parents had come from. But I didn't go there.

My revulsion against everything German went so far that I didn't even want to go to Tel Aviv when I visited Israel because the German emigrés all lived in Tel Aviv.

But then things changed. Apparently we can't escape our fate. In Greece I met a group of young people from Berlin who were terribly nice, and we exchanged addresses. Then I visited a friend in Zurich and the two of us decided to go to Berlin. On the train we shared a compartment with two other passengers— an old peasant from Bavaria and a young man. I spoke hardly any German, my friend spoke only Yiddish, and the old peasant an almost incomprehensible local patois. But somehow we managed to carry on a conversation, to the amusement of the young man. He is now my husband—a non-Jew, a German— and the father of my daughter.

I have studied psychology, and a wealth of interpretations and fantasies offer themselves to describe this situation. But why elaborate? The reality is fantastic enough. On my first trip through this country in which my parents were mistreated, humiliated, and finally driven out, and in which other relatives were murdered, I met a man who is a child of those who committed these monstrous deeds and fell in love with him.

On this first trip through Germany I also visited my mother's village. It was a terrible experience. A farm family who had lived

I Couldn't Have Survived

across the street now lived in my mother's house. The first thing they showed me was the Jewish cemetery, very pleasant and friendly, the way one shows a visiting stranger the sights. I was a guest in my mother's house. I stayed for dinner, barely able to swallow the food, unable to put down the thought that these people were sitting on my chairs, were offering me a piece of my bread, and that I was even expected to be grateful.

I spent the night at an inn and left the next morning.

Yet despite these experiences my return to the land of my ancestors was inevitable. Some weeks later my boy friend visited me in New York and stayed for a few weeks, and I then decided to return to Germany with him. By coincidence I got a job as a teacher in Berlin. My parents knew nothing about my boy friend. As far as they were concerned I was there because of the chance to teach in that particular school. Even after I was already living with him in Germany I had to make up stories. At the time I wouldn't have dared tell them that he was a German, and a non-Jew to boot. I told them that the telephone number I gave them belonged to a neighbor who would call me to the phone. But after six months this whole arrangement struck me as so crazy that I married him. That same day I called my parents, and we had a hilarious conversation. I told my mother that I had just married a German guy, and she yelled back at me, "What, you've just married a German goy?" And she was right. When I told her his name, she said with a note of surprise, "But isn't that your neighbor with the telephone?"

Eventually they accepted it. Later my mother told me that perhaps it was a good thing I hadn't said anything earlier, because if I had she might have committed suicide. But my husband also ran into problems. His family are devout Catholics. His parents, thank God, weren't Nazis. But when he told them that he planned to marry, the only thing they asked him was whether I was a Protestant. When he said no, they were happy. But then when he told them that I wasn't Catholic either, but Jewish, they really flipped. That was impossible, they said; it meant we couldn't have a church wedding.

But all of them eventually calmed down. A few weeks later my parents came to Germany to meet my in-laws. I was terribly nervous before that meeting. But it went off far better than what I had expected. The door opened, the parents looked at each other and fell into each others' arms. The mothers cried, and all of them said, "Now how about our children, aren't they something!"

It was very moving. They got along from the very beginning. Never a word about the past; they were just happy; reconciled, satisfied, and happy.

At the time I always said that I would stay in Germany three years at the most. After that I would go back to America. But even then my husband asked me what if I liked it here. "That doesn't matter," I'd answer. "Regardless of how much I like it, after three years I go back." Meanwhile almost fifteen years have passed and I'm still in Germany, and it looks as though I'll stay. And in recent years everything has become much better; I feel much more comfortable than in the beginning.

I had some bad times during those first years, above all because I didn't speak German too well. There were always arguments—in the subway, at the grocer's, often because of ridiculous little things, about whether one was supposed to get on the bus in the front or the back, whether the fruit could be handled, or whether there was an extra charge for a plastic bag. I would get into a rage and come home in tears. As far as I was concerned they were all the murderers of my grandparents, and if they could they would do the same to me. I was angry but also disappointed, and I was certain that nothing in Germany had

I Couldn't Have Survived

changed. That first year I also wanted to attend Rosh Hashanah services. I thought, you're living here in Germany with a non-Jew, are lying to your parents, the least you can do is go to the synagogue. But when I got there, they wouldn't let me in. They asked for a seat ticket, and I didn't have one. I was shocked. That couldn't have happened in New York. People would have moved together, and they would have found a seat for me. No one would have been kept out. But here! First German, then Jewish! That also played a crucial role in my break with the Community here. I was no longer interested in becoming more closely involved with these people. I also felt I wasn't a part of them.

Then my daughter was born. From the outset I had decided to bring her up as a Jew. I just wouldn't let her become a German. But it wasn't all that simple. On the one hand I had no contact with the Community, and on the other hand the Jewish kindergarten and its teaching methods were so at odds with my ideas that the entire burden of my decision rested on me. In recent years I've met other Jews who also don't belong to the Community yet follow Jewish tradition. We now celebrate the holidays together, and I am happy to have found them. I told my daughter, who knows about all the other holidays like Christmas from kindergarten, that some people celebrate some holidays, and other people celebrate others. Her reaction to this was cute. The Jews have it best, she said, they can celebrate all the holidays. But still, despite everything, I don't feel comfortable here in Germany. I still have my American passport and I'd like to have a whole lot of other passports as well. Then I could leave here with my daughter anytime I wanted, just pick her up, leave everything here, and take the next plane. I am afraid above all for my daughter. The thought that someone might take her away from me is terrifying. Perhaps this fear will die down in fifteen or twenty years, but as long as even one person of that time is still alive . . . Still, my fear of war is greater than my fear of anti-Semitism.

I've had some pretty bad experiences here in Germany, mostly with older people. Because of my dark hair and eyes I am often taken for Turkish. Then I get to hear all sorts of slurs. When I first came here, when I still had some problems with the language and couldn't defend myself so well, I always carried a slip of paper with a list of insults. And when someone made some stupid remarks I'd read off the list.

Once I also threw an acquaintance of my husband out of the house. I had come home in a state because I had been mistaken for a Turk and been insulted, and I told them about it, so our visitor became indignant at my being treated like a Turk. She couldn't understand why I got furious and threw her out. It didn't occur to her that her indignation showed contempt for Turks. Another one, a woman of thirty, told me that she wasn't responsible for what had happened here before her time. I can't accept that. If Goethe and Beethoven are part of German history, then so are Hitler and Goering.

In the meantime I've learned somehow to handle all the prejudices and repressions here, and also to defend myself. But the fear and the rage remain. I can try to keep my eyes open and recognize a future danger in its earliest stages in order to escape in time. But what happens if I miss the right moment? I used to tell myself that survival is possible even under the worst conditions and that somewhere I would find the strength to survive. That word *somewhere* was a consolation, or a tranquilizer. I told myself I'd manage somehow to get myself and my daughter through. After all, I'd spent my life with survivors—those who fled and the handful who even survived the camps.

Who can visualize death, whether it's death in a concentra-

I Couldn't Have Survived

tion camp or on the way to the camp or in prison? So few survived, but they give us, the postwar generation, the feeling that it would have been possible to escape the slaughter. By keeping silent they also deprive us of their experiences.

But since then I've had a sobering experience. A few years ago a film about the Nazis was being made here. A notice posted on the bulletin board of the Jewish Community said they needed extras who looked Jewish. I thought nothing of it and applied. We were dressed in camp uniforms as part of a camp scene. It was absolutely absurd. Jews playing Jews in a picture about persecuted Jews, courtesy of the Jewish Community.

Everything was as it had been then. We were given shovels and were supposed to dig a ditch. In front of us stood SS soldiers shouting at us as we worked, everything just playacting. The scenes had to be shot over and over again until the director was satisfied that they were realistic enough. And then I realized that I would never have survived the torture and abuse. I would have been among the first to perish. After half an hour of shoveling, I was utterly exhausted, and I spent three weeks in bed with bronchitis.

I somehow have to find a way to live here with my family, have a home, and still remain sharp-witted enough to know when it's time to leave. I want my daughter to attend the American school. I don't want her to feel that she's nothing but a German. She has American citizenship as well. The American school will most likely also have some Jewish students, and that will give her some contact with that part of her past.

But what will finally become of her I can't say. All I can do is try to influence her to preserve her Jewish identity, because I now consider myself neither an American nor a German. I am a Jew.

6

David

Nothing Can Happen to Me Here

MY GRANDMOTHER on my mother's side is still alive. My grandfather is missing, somewhere in Russia, I've been told. So much for my mother's parents. My father's father supposedly spent the war years in Germany hidden in some bunker reading until he lost his sight. By the time the war ended he was blind. Some time later he died, I don't know when. I never saw either of my grandfathers. Actually I have no idea who they were, what they did, and where they came from.

I know a little more about my grandmothers. My mother's mother, for example, never took Judaism very seriously. Maybe that's why she survived.

But in fact I know very little about my parents' generation. How come? I've no idea. Everything happened a long time ago.

I was born here in Berlin, in 1969. I've always lived here, and now I'm in the tenth grade. Until recently Judaism was never a big topic of discussion in our family. It was always taken for granted that one goes to temple—every Friday, Yom Kippur, and all the other holidays. That was quite normal for me. But I can't say that I always liked going. My mother wanted it, and I went along without giving it much thought. The preservation of tradition didn't mean as much to me as to my mother. And furthermore, I don't believe in God. I am a scientist, I'm interested in technology and mathematics, and they stand in contradiction to religious belief. So all that's left is tradition. But that alone doesn't make a person a Jew. Anyway, it's not enough for me. It was always the same at the synagogue. Nothing I saw there convinced me that I am or should be a Jew. What's the point of it all? I never got an answer to that. I am and will remain a Jew even without the synagogue. I simply have no feeling of belonging there; I don't feel like part of the majority. I stand around and wait until everything is over. Emotionally nothing much happens there. Sure, I know others my age who don't feel the same way at all. But I can't force myself to feel something that just isn't there.

I went to the Jewish kindergarten and also belonged to the Jewish youth group. A lot of the kids there never questioned anything. They probably came from Orthodox families, where one doesn't question or fight anything. For them everything was always so simple and logical. In some ways things are probably easier for them than for me. The belief and tradition were handed down to the children automatically and the children are as religious as the parents. I also don't go to the German Zionist Youth Club. At first I didn't even know what they did there, and now that I know I certainly don't go. I once met a group leader of the Zionist Youth. He had chaperoned the sports group to which I still go. One evening we were sitting around when out of the blue he asked me whether I had already reached a decision about going to Israel after graduating from high school.

"What do you mean?" I asked him. "I'm not going to Israel after graduation. I live here in Berlin and want to stay here." He seemed surprised and suggested that I go to the Zionist Youth. All the people there were going to Israel after they graduated.

I've had enough. Enough of the Zionist Youth, of youth leaders, and most of all of their superior and patronizing attitude toward other Jews who aren't in the Zionist Youth. They think they're the elite of the elite. Just being Jewish isn't enough by itself. There are even higher-ranking Jews, namely those in the Zionist Youth. The people there also close themselves off from others, go to the club every day, and don't want to know anybody else. All they talk about is Israel. But the funny thing is that I heard from the older members that they don't go to Israel after graduating either. They just talk big and think they're something special. Anyway, I don't feel at home or very comfortable there. They're Jews, but they don't accept me as much as my non-Jewish friends do, who at least leave me in peace about Israel. What do I have to do with that country? Perhaps in the back of my mind, way back, something stirs. But otherwise it's a country like any other.

I like going to the Jewish sports club. There these things aren't discussed. We train and play our games, and often our opponents don't even know that we're a Jewish team. We're just some club with a funny name. Nobody thinks about Jews. And when they ask us what Maccabee means we tell them, and most of the time they are surprised. At most they see Jews only on TV, and never any Jewish athletes. They know nothing about Jews, never see any, and if they ever heard anything at all it was about the extermination under the Nazis.

It isn't easy to be consciously Jewish in Germany. Lately I haven't been going to temple as much. It wasn't a spontaneous decision, but I am debating whether I should continue to go at all. I want to be a Jew without obligations and advantages. I'd like to go to school on the Sabbath and on Yom Kippur like all the others. I don't want all these restrictions that separate me from the others. Of course it would be different if there were a lot of Jews here who all did the same thing. But that's not how it is.

I'm the only one in my class who stays at home on Yom Kippur. When I go back the next day I say, "Sorry, I couldn't come to school yesterday because it was Yom Kippur." Then they all look at me stupidly, and I have to explain—to the teachers, to the class—always justifying myself and explaining why, what it's all about. I don't want that. I want to live like all the others. Not that I'm afraid of the kids and the teachers, they know that I'm a Jew. But I don't want to have any special privileges. If they have to go to school then I should go too. I'll still be a Jew anyway. And I even like being part of a minority. It makes me a little bit special. But basically I'm like anybody else, like a Christian or a Moslem or a Hindu. We also have a Moslem in our class. There's nothing different about him except for his name. He plays soccer as good or as bad as the others, takes his exams, and picks his nose. He doesn't want to be or to think of himself as anything special. He also never talks about going to Iran or some such place after graduating. He lives his life like his German classmates. He is a Berliner just like me.

If I had to rank what I am, I'd say Berliner, Jew, German, in that order. German last, because I have no relationship to Germany. What's there to Germany except Berlin? I'm not a patriot, but I would like to stay here in Berlin.

Marry a Jewish woman? That wouldn't be important to me. Whether she's Christian or any other religion means nothing. I'd also treat my children like that. They should decide for themselves whether they want to follow tradition or not. Perhaps

I'll even marry a Christian and let them be baptized. Anything is possible. I'd have no qualms. Of course I'd tell my children about my past, take them to temple and hand on to them what I know, even though it's not much. Sometimes I'm sorry that I know so little. If it happens that my children are Jews, and that depends on the mother, let them observe or not, as they wish. They should find their own Judaism, not have it handed down by others. Perhaps I'll see things differently when I get older. I don't want to say that my ideas will remain unchanged for all time. I am looking for a new way, a way that lets me be a Jew without constantly obeying rules laid down by others. Sometimes I also wonder what would happen if everything were like it was before—the racism, the hatred of Jews. I don't know what I'd do if, for example, my school friends were to call me a Jew and tell me that they wouldn't play with me any more.

I can't imagine that it could happen again and don't even want to think about it. I must admit there's a little fear. I see the hatred of foreigners in the population, and that could take a nasty turn. But the government, no, I don't think so. They would quickly intercede, and on our behalf. They'd protect us, I'm certain of that. They wouldn't allow a recurrence of the Holocaust. Neither would the other countries. If the Germans were to start up again, the whole world would be up in arms.

Still I know it could get that bad again, despite my optimism. In such a situation I wouldn't run away immediately. I'd act like anybody else; I'd stop going to the synagogue and refrain from any provocation. Some others would undoubtedly continue to go to temple and observe their rituals. But they are the very Orthodox who want to show how firmly they cling to Judaism. I wouldn't do that. I'd sooner pull back and give up everything Jewish. I don't want to leave here. I like it here. It would be terrible if I had to flee like a criminal.

Nothing Can Happen to Me Here

That is really my only great fear, to have to leave this city, to be forced to leave. There is a trend in Germany now. If the Germans begin to feel like Germans again and if Germans were the only ones living here in Germany, things could become unpleasant.

I don't think that a persecution of Jews could happen again here in Germany, but if it should, the Jews again wouldn't defend themselves. Most of the grown-ups I know have become so rich and so cocky they'd never believe that anybody could move against them. They would calmly wait until they were killed. They'd see it as their lot to die as Jews, except for the few leftists and intellectuals who have a broader view—like Berliners, who all have a broader view. Those few types who do not belong to the official Community and who live their own lives as Jews are the resistance fighters of the future. They too don't believe in God but would fight for Judaism. That's my aspiration, to be a Jew without believing in God. The men in the synagogue with their black suits, mumbling to themselves, what have they to do with me? They're as foreign to me as the followers of any other religion.

And the young people who speak to me in Hebrew and make a long face when I can't understand them, who let me feel that they despise me. What are they? The children of rich parents. And what did they do to earn it? Nothing. Why are they so stuck-up? I can do without that sort of Jewishness. If they're unable to accept their own brothers and sisters, then the hell with them.

They are like that man on the other side I heard about, who supposedly said, "I decide who's a Jew!"

In that case I'd rather be a Jew according to my own lights, even without the others.

7

Helene

I Have a Dream

I HAVE A DREAM, a recurring dream, and not just when I sleep. It is always with me, day and night. I dream of leading a life as a Jew, as an observant Jewish woman, with all that it involves, all the advantages and disadvantages, without regard for my so-called normal environment. I would like to live like my ancestors, but in the present. I don't want to crawl into some hole, to withdraw or retreat into some Orthodox group in Israel. I want to lead a normal life as a Jew here in Austria or in some other European country, or even in Israel—live in a city doing work I like, but as a Jew to whom Jewish laws are more important than the feelings and expectations of my environment.

Of course I'd have a Jewish husband, and he would be as observant as I was, for otherwise I couldn't live with him. It would be a life of laws and rituals, a strict life, but it would neither restrict nor impede us. On the contrary, it would enable us to follow a five-thousand-year-old tradition that should not be allowed to come to a sudden end. That, I believe, is our task and our responsibility.

I didn't always have this dream. And my parents are no example when it comes to this. True, they go to temple on holidays, but they treat it more like a meeting place for seeing old friends than as a religious ritual. That's how I feel about most of the people at the synagogue. Sometimes on the Sabbath I sit there and look at the men standing around in groups of two or three, talking softly, hardly ever looking at the cantor in front. Then I ask myself, "Why are they meeting here? They could just as well have gone to a bar." Recently I confronted my father with this. He, too, stands around there talking with friends. He responded by giving me a lecture. He began by explaining to me that one of the functions of the synagogue was to make it possible for Jews in the Diaspora to have a meeting place, that my vision of the temple only as a site of prayer would diminish its role—that's what makes it different from the Christian church. It all sounded very learned and academic, but it didn't change anything in his distance from belief and religious Judaism.

Both my parents were born in Israel—my father in 1940, my mother in 1944. All my grandparents came from Vienna. They returned to Austria in the fifties, I don't know exactly why. We never talk about it. When I once asked my parents why they left Israel, they reacted very aggressively. My grandparents had had a very hard life there, they said, the grandfathers were forever serving in the army, and the specter of war was always present. Who could live under such conditions? But when I yelled at my father, "Is it easier to live here in Austria among potential murderers?," he got up without a word and left the room. My mother then turned on me and demanded that I apologize. But I didn't. The subject has never been mentioned again.

Both my sets of grandparents were in the textile business before emigrating from Vienna. My father's parents in particular I think were quite prosperous. They probably could never get used to their modest circumstances in Israel. Here in Vienna they soon worked their way up again. My father has now taken over their business; my mother stays at home.

We can be considered well-to-do. We have a lovely house, take at least one big trip a year, and I get pretty much everything I want. We lack nothing, and still there is an emptiness around us. We're sitting in a gilded cage, beautifully furnished, and the little door leading out can be opened at will, but it's still a cage, with too much food in it.

When I was little I wanted for nothing. If my parents didn't give it to me my grandparents did. The most beautiful clothes, the most expensive bicycle, music lessons, ballet lessons, the best the city had to offer. My parents don't do these things out of ostentation, to show off what we have and who we are. And they're not chasing after the most expensive and most unusual. No, I think they just enjoy the feeling of being able to afford anything they want. I can tell that they're having fun. They live for the moment. My mother once told me to enjoy life as long as they let me. I am beginning to understand what she meant by it. Both my parents live as though the Nazis could return any day. But neither of them, neither my father nor my mother, has faith in God anymore. And that's what I can't understand. Both of them grew up in the land of our fathers, in that country where it is easier to be Jewish than anywhere else on earth. But they lost it, their belief, here in Austria.

I can remember when I was small my father still was the first one to get up in the morning to help form a minyan. And if for some reason he failed to show up, the others would call up to find out what was wrong, whether he was sick or something.

I Have a Dream

And we also used to go to the synagogue Friday night and Saturday morning. But today they only go on the High Holy Days, on Yom Kippur and Rosh Hashanah. It has become a routine, a habit. I don't want to live like my mother, and I want my future husband to take his Jewishness more seriously than my father does.

Two years ago, at my bat mitzvah, everything changed for me. That's when I decided that I wouldn't live like my parents. That's when my girl friend Ruth and I—we're in the same class and sit next to each other—began to observe the laws. Our parents were in shock. We announced that we wouldn't go to school on Saturday. One Friday evening, I remember it exactly, it was January and freezing cold, we went to the synagogue and both of us swore not only to be Jews but to become observant, believing Jews. It was a sacred oath, and we agreed to help each other stand fast. At the same time we told our parents that from now on we would observe the Sabbath. At first my father ridiculed us. What will you do on the Sabbath? No radio, stereo, or TV? No moped rides to the city, no tennis in the summer, no movies? But Ruth and I didn't budge. For the past two years she and I have been going to synagogue on Friday nights and on Saturday; we take walks and visit each other, talk or read to each other. The Sabbath has become the most beautiful day in the week for us. No diversions, no outside entertainment—nothing distracts us on that day.

After a few weeks, when my parents realized how important this day was for me, they got together with Ruth's parents. They consulted about what to do. Then followed a painful discussion among all of us—my parents, Ruth, and her parents. They tried to persuade us that there were different ways of living like a Jew, that the old rituals were not suited to our times, that we would suffer at school, and more such nonsense.

Ruth and I were furious, and we were also astonished at the insensitivity of our parents. We cried and spoke of leaving home, of going to a kibbutz in Israel where at least we could live as Jews. Both our parents then backed off and tried to calm us down. They accepted our feelings about the Sabbath even though they didn't understand us.

The next step was that we stopped eating pork. That got hardly any reaction from our parents. My father just made some cynical remarks about whether I couldn't be religious like Christians, who do everything quietly, without tyrannizing the entire neighborhood. He at any rate wouldn't give up his pork chops. I could eat them or leave them, which I did. In Ruth's house it was the same. She simply didn't eat half the food served there.

In school we decided to change the way we behaved. We refused to be the information center about Judaism. Before, whenever the topic of Judaism came up, we were it. True, the teachers meant well, they didn't intend anything anti-Jewish. But whether Israel was being discussed in our geography class, or the Nazis, in history, or Heinrich Heine, in German, we were the ones called on. If Einstein was mentioned in physics, or Mendelssohn in music, they all looked at us. See, again one of yours, their expressions said. And they were always pleased, almost proud, to have one of "those" in their class. After all, there are so-o-o few of them left in Vienna, and we even have two of them! And we were asked about what we eat at home, how we celebrate Christmas or why we don't, what we do instead, whether everybody in Israel really observes the Sabbath, whether Heine was a good or bad Jew because he converted, why some men cover their heads, and why the women sit separately in the synagogue.

A few years ago I was still happy to tell them about these

I Have a Dream

things. But now I'm too proud. I don't want to be a living museum anymore, and I also don't want to be a museum guide explaining strange and exotic practices, constantly having to talk about things others don't understand and never will understand. I don't ask any of them why their grandfather was in the SS or why their grandmother went on bike trips with the League of German Girls while my grandfather was spat on in the street and his business taken from him. They are Austrians, non-Jews, and children of the Nazis—strangers three times over. And the teachers often reacted even more peculiarly than the students. When Ruth once described what she felt when she was sitting up in the balcony in the synagogue with the women, the teacher didn't even go into Ruth's experience but instead talked about the oppression of women through religion. She told the class that certain religions—Islam and Judaism—were extremely hostile to women, as demonstrated by the separation of men and women in the synagogue and the veiling of women in Islam. Ruth and I were indignant. We asked her, "When did the Jews ever burn women as witches, as the Christians did?" But she persisted, and so we got up and left the room. All hell broke loose, our parents were called, and finally our teacher apologized to us, said it was a misunderstanding, but we didn't believe a word she said. The principal probably made her apologize.

I don't know what the future looks like. More than anything I would like to live in a kosher household. Of course I don't want to leave my parents, but if I marry I would like my husband to take the Jewish tradition seriously. I don't want to become like my parents, who remember their tradition only when a famous artist or scientist turns out to have been Jewish. I can do without that sort of pride. That's not much different from the Austrians and Germans, who see us only as a people of artists and merchants, not as believers in God.

But most of my parents' friends are like that. They romanticize their type of Jewishness, are proud of minor differences like their dark hair or dark complexion or different mentality. But being Jewish without awe of God? A house or a bar of gold can be left to your heirs, but an identity, a communality? That is something you have to achieve on your own. The fact that my parents and grandparents are Jews is only one part, perhaps even the least significant part, of my personality. I could have gone over to Judaism even if I'd had entirely different parents. And I see it as my task to hand on this tradition. In Vienna there are Jewish communities that take the laws far more seriously than the official one. Those are the ones I feel drawn to. I will bring up my children as Jews and give them religious support. Then it won't matter to them whether they live in Israel, Austria, or wherever. They will find their community wherever they are, and with it their home. I'm tired of my parents' discussions about whether it is better to live in Austria or outside. When their friends visit, the talk is always the same: whether they should leave or not, and how bad things are here, that they feel persecuted and are afraid of a new anti-Semitism.

None of them realize that what they lack is the support of religious belief. And they have no idea how alien one feels here if one lives as a real Jew. Only since Ruth and I have tried to take the Jewish laws seriously have we become aware of the lack of understanding all around us.

One time, when school didn't begin until 10 o'clock, we went to a café for breakfast. We ordered soft-boiled eggs, coffee, rolls, and so on. When Ruth cracked her egg she found a blood spot. We didn't know exactly what to do, but finally we agreed that eating it was not allowed. We called the waitress and asked for another egg. She asked what was wrong. We explained to her that as pious Jews we couldn't eat the egg because of the speck of blood. She was puzzled, didn't know what to say, but she removed the egg without saying anything and a few minutes later brought another one. But during the whole time we sat there eating, she kept on looking over to us and whispering with the other help, who also kept looking at us.

But we were proud. We were glad that we'd had the courage to send the egg back and to openly show our Jewishness. It was like a symbolic act for us. Since then we tell it to everybody without worrying whether we're stepping on anyone's toes. We will always be Jews, no matter where we are and with whom. And if that's so, let's do it right!

8

Robert and Erika

I Don't Share Your Yearning

ROBERT: We've been living together for five years. We have a four-year-old daughter. Erika is a teacher, I'm a doctor. I am Jewish, Erika isn't. We're not married. We've been talking about getting married for the past two years, but we always find a reason not to. And I'm not always the one to come up with it. Erika, too, is sometimes for it and sometimes not. So it isn't that I don't marry her because she isn't Jewish. It may look like it, but it isn't so.

ERIKA: I am Austrian. I was born in Linz and moved to Vienna to finish college. I'm an ordinary Austrian. Nothing about me is exotic, strange, or foreign. My parents come from Upper Austria, and so do my grandparents. I met Robert in a café. I noticed him because of his looks, his dark, curly hair, his brown eyes. I was attracted to him. When I saw him it didn't occur to me that he might be a Jew or a foreigner. During the early months of our love, neither his nor my background was an

I Don't Share Your Yearning

issue. At some point he told me that he was Jewish, and my reaction was something like, so what? For me during those first exciting weeks he was simply my Robert. Nothing else mattered, and nothing would have made any difference. He could have been the son of an SS officer or of a murdered Jew. I was in love with him.

ROBERT: That's true. The way you tell it, that was really the most beautiful time of our relationship. Everything was so untroubled. We were so lighthearted. But we couldn't run fast enough; the past was bound to catch up with us. There came a time when we began to talk about our parents. And there came the time when my parents wanted to meet Erika. For days I went around with the intention of telling her about my parents, and them about Erika. But I was too cowardly. Above all I didn't have the courage to tell my parents about her.

ERIKA: He told me about it only at the very last minute, on the way to his parents. But as far as I was concerned, all these precautions were unnecessary, because as I said, at the time it didn't matter to me. But for Robert's parents it was a shock, and so it also turned into a shock for me. I won't forget that evening so soon. Up to then I'd never had any contact with Jews. Linz, where I grew up, didn't exactly offer very many opportunities for that.

We came to the apartment, rang the bell, his father opened the door—and stared at us. I, the blonde from the sticks, pure Aryan, of an—as I have since learned—impeccably anti-Semitic family, standing there with his son, his only son. What happened then was a mixture of strangeness and embarrassment. Some of Robert's relatives were there, too, about ten people in all, and I was the only non-Jew. But I was so curious about this scene that was so strange to me that I wasn't even aware of their reaction to me. Everything there was different from my home. The men had their heads covered even while they ate. There was ceaseless talk, arguments, even shouting, without anyone getting mad, and throughout it all the stereo was playing at top volume. The children were allowed to do whatever they pleased. Instead of sitting quietly at the table, the way they did at my house, they climbed up on the laps of their grandfathers and uncles without anyone reprimanding them. It was total chaos. The men sat next to the men and the women next to the women, instead of man, woman, man, woman, as was the custom at my house. I found myself in a completely alien world. I tried to understand what was going on here, in the middle of Vienna, in the apartment of the parents of my boyfriend, my Robert, who until now had seemed as ordinary to me as any other friend. And suddenly all my curiosity, all admiration, vanished. I was overcome by a terrible premonition that I would lose this man without ever having had him. I felt as though I were standing behind a sheet of glass separating us from each other. And suddenly I became aware that no one at this gathering had spoken a single word to me. All of them were laughing and shouting and I sat there and was ignored. They looked past me, spoke past me; no one ever looked directly at me. The rest of the evening was like a wake for me. I tried to talk to Robert at least, but whenever I found myself near him somebody would take his arm and pull him away, as if they had something important to tell him, something that couldn't wait. And Robert let himself be dragged away. He did nothing to make that evening tolerable for me.

ROBERT: We've talked about that evening hundreds of times, and my version never agrees with yours. It wasn't directed against you. It was an evening with my family, and on that evening my family was more important to me than you. It had nothing to do with my love for you, and you know it.

ERIKA: But the evening with my parents some weeks later was

I Don't Share Your Yearning

entirely different. You were the focal point. Everything centered on you, the guest. My parents didn't ignore you; on the contrary. They asked you questions and talked to you. As far as my parents were concerned, you were my friend, and they accepted you as a part of me.

ROBERT: They didn't accept me. They were scared stiff. You yourself asked me before we got there not to bring up the Nazis, because your father would talk all kinds of garbage and you and your mother were afraid of that. And your father? He sat there, this former SS officer, and he was shaking in his boots, afraid that I would ask him about it. And our so-called pleasant, friendly conversation was about the weather, food, and wine.

ERIKA: Better small talk than what happened next, when you suddenly felt compelled to bring up the Kristallnacht in Linz, when Jewish women were publicly raped and the Gestapo had to intervene to protect the Jews from the rabid Austrians. What did you expect? That it would lead to an interesting discussion about the Nazi era in Austria?

ROBERT: I only spoke the truth. As your favorite writer, Ingeborg Bachmann, put it, one ought to be able to expect people to face up to the truth. But your situation is typical of an entire generation here in Austria. As children of the '68 movement you were big antifascists, made passionate speeches attacking the neo-Nazis, marched in every demonstration. But at home with your own parents? There the big protest stopped. The "Nazi swine," as you had previously called them, turned into an ailing, weak father and a mother bent in pain who had trouble walking. "Why torture them?" you asked. Contempt gave way to pity. And everything they had done was suddenly forgotten or put on the back burner.

ERIKA: What do you want me to do? Hate my parents? Should I kill my father for what he did? I couldn't choose my parents. Believe me, I'd much rather have a father who had behaved differently during the war. An unbroken relationship to the past is nothing but a pipe dream.

ROBERT: What do you mean unbroken? There was a time when you were filled with hatred and contempt for your parents. Now, a few years later, it has given way to understanding. As if one could ever understand what they did. Just because your father now has trouble breathing and a bad leg, that doesn't change anything; he still behaved like a swine back then.

ERIKA: It's easy for you to talk. But what do you have to do with the fact that your parents were victims? Did you help them survive the concentration camp? Or were you perhaps born in the camp? What gives you the right to insult my father? Your parents might possibly have that right, but you? Go and avenge yourself someplace else, not with me.

ROBERT: My parents spent three years in Dachau, my mother's parents were murdered in Auschwitz, my father's parents were sent to a ghetto in Eastern Europe and he never heard from them again. At the very most, ten of my other relatives survived. Before the war there were a hundred and fifty of them. My mother has to wear a wig because she lost her hair in the camp and it won't grow back. When I was a little boy I heard my father scream in his sleep. Every one of my parents' friends has a story to tell filled with tragedy and catastrophe. And you ask me what my parents' past has to do with me? The past was always the present, can't you understand that? It was always with us, not just in stories about the past. And how were things with you? How often did your parents tell you how their Jewish neighbors fared?

ERIKA: All right, all right, I didn't want to hurt you. But just think, just look at what's been happening to you in recent years. More and more you're rejecting everything connected with me,

I Don't Share Your Yearning

whether it's my family or my friends, and at the same time you've begun to turn to your own background. As paradoxical as it may sound, our love seems to have reawakened your interest in Jewishness. When I first met you, you weren't like your father. Synagogue, Jewish holidays, none of it was particularly important to you. And now? Unfortunately, your turning toward Judaism also contains an element of exclusion. I sometimes have the feeling that I'm no longer good enough for you. You want a certified Jewish woman. I can feel that you're drawing away. Suddenly you started to go to the synagogue, and at the same time you stopped visiting my parents. You began to find my friends and colleagues repulsive. At parties you sit in a corner without talking, or you pick a fight. What do you want of me? How many people do I have to reject in order to be fair to you? My parents, my friends, everybody?

ROBERT: Your friends! Your friends! You know very well what has become of them. These so-called progressives of unexceptionable political credentials, leftist or at least liberal, who supposedly had discarded all forms of racism and inhumanity like an old shirt. But they can't fool me. The past is etched into their skin. I've seen the difference between what they say and what they do. Just think of your friend Emil, that leftist journalist, who invited us to his parents' house. There sat his father in the living room, holding forth while his mother slaved away in the kitchen, served the meal, and then disappeared without sitting down to eat with us. Like a housemaid. And the son? Not a word to his mother, but stupid man-to-man talk with his father. Or Ferdinand, another one of your journalist friends, delivering his lectures all over the place, critical talks which he introduces with an anti-Semitic joke about the word *chutzpah*, a joke that dates back to the Nazis. And he's not even aware of what he's saying. He has no feeling for it. They can't fool me with their trendy talk. I don't trust them. In their eyes I see reflected the brutality and cruelty of their parents, with whom they spent so many years of their lives. How I had wanted to be accepted by them, but instead I was exploited and rejected. Today I'm glad that I have my own medical practice. The patients come to me because they expect to be helped. I treat all of them, regardless of whether they're Nazis or Communists. To me they're not individuals but sick people, sick bodies brought to me for repair. I concentrate on their disorders and shut out everything else. But as perverse as that may sound, they all depend on me. None of them is superior to me, or even my equal. They put themselves into my care as soon as they set foot in my office. The power now belongs to me. This is the only profession for me here in Vienna in this situation, and it is the only reason I'm still here.

ERIKA: If everybody here is your enemy, why don't you go to Israel? Why do you torture yourself with having to live here, and why do you also torture me with it?

ROBERT: That's all you can ever say when I get worked up about the situation here. But I don't go to Israel, just as you don't go to Russia, which you've always been told to do when you criticize things here. But on one point you're right. My life with you was the impetus for my return to my roots. But I never felt that this was directed against you.

ERIKA: Oh, no, not against me! You despise my parents, you don't want to see my friends anymore, you claim that the leftists here, of whom I consider myself one, are the same kind of anti-Semites as the right-wingers, you think of my people—and they *are* my people—as a bunch of madmen and murderers. You see only your Jewish friends. Only *your* family is a regular part of our lives. We visit your parents regularly, your sisters call up every day, we have to interrupt our skiing vacation because

I Don't Share Your Yearning

an uncle from Israel is visiting Vienna. Only your people, your decent, morally impeccable circle, with no black marks on their past. And what's left for me?

True, I could convert to Judaism. But you've got to understand! I am a descendant of the criminals, and what I am looking for is reconciliation, not a change of allegiance. I'm no turncoat. I try to reach out, not in order to become your accomplice against my past but to begin again, free of murderers and victims. But in recent months you've left me no room for reconciliation. You have hardened and withdrawn from me.

ROBERT: I can forget the guilt, but not the guilty. I can tell myself over and over again that the persecution of Jews is nothing new, that it wasn't invented by the Nazis. But I'm not broad-minded enough to accept your father's role in the mass execution of women and children. And it was done by individuals—by Frau Maier, the camp guard, and by Herr Mueller, the judge. With them there can be no reconciliation. I cannot hold out my right hand to them when their left hand still holds the bloodstained knife. What do you expect of me?

ERIKA: Not everybody feels the way you do. After 1945 many Communists who had been persecuted just like the Jews returned to Vienna, and they helped in the reconstruction of this country. Or look at Kreisky, a Jew, who has even tried to halt Simon Wiesenthal's campaign of vengeance.

ROBERT: They all belong to a different generation.

ERIKA: Yes, they all experienced the suffering personally and didn't grow up like you here, in peace and prosperity.

ROBERT: My parents' generation was in a state of shock after the war. They lived out their remaining years paralyzed, forever wedded to the state of terror. They were incapable of reacting to what had happened; all they wanted was to forget. But I was born after that reign of terror. I learned about the horror of the

Nazi era without letting it paralyze my brain. I can hate again, and that's good. And I despise all the Jews who after the war helped this country to cleanse itself. Especially in Vienna, where there's so little guilt or repentance, these Jews, by pretending that everything is over, bless the murderers of their families. They murder them all over again. But I also despise all those folkloristic festivals now being held in Vienna that celebrate the Jewish past in Austria. The emcees hand each other lists of names of incinerated corpses, so as not to lose track as they reminisce about the good old days. And I also despise the representatives of my generation who now serve as living exhibits to help refute the reality of the final solution. They let themselves be celebrated as survivors by their executioners, who toast them at dinners and receptions and are not ashamed. Sometimes I don't know who despises us more, we ourselves or the others.

ERIKA: Is there anybody whom you don't despise? Show me someone you don't hate.

ROBERT: The pious, Orthodox Jews, they're the ones I admire. They keep faith with their God regardless of what country they live in and under what dictators. Even in the concentration camps, under the most terrible conditions, they still tried to live according to their faith. My father also has talked about it. But the others? One day they might even get the notion of wearing a Jewish star so that they can be readily identified as Jews and remind their non-Jewish neighbors of their guilt. They expect special treatment because their ancestors were murdered. They want to be rewarded because their parents survived. They don't want to fight their potential murderers, because they'd rather be indulged and spoiled by them. In Vienna, if need be, one makes arrangements even with the murderers of one's own parents.

ERIKA: I ask myself what's to become of our daughter. According to your laws she's not Jewish. In my eyes she's at least half-Jewish. I don't want her to become like my parents, but something within me balks at bringing her up as a Jew. I couldn't help her there, I'm not Jewish. I cannot impose on her an identity that is alien to me.

ROBERT: We could send her to the Jewish school in Vienna . . .

ERIKA: What part of me will then be part of her? Everything she learns there will be directed against me. I don't know Hebrew, don't understand her prayers, and don't even know how Hanukkah is celebrated. You didn't teach me how to become a Jewish mother. Until recently you were a Jew of the past. Your Jewishness lay in mourning the dead and anger at the murderers. You celebrated all your traditions outside our relationship. In our home there was no trace of your religion and your laws. We celebrated Christmas, and at Hanukkah you went to your parents, up to now supposedly only as a favor to them. But now you've begun to bring your suddenly rediscovered, redefined identity into our family. But it hasn't enriched our family life. On the contrary, it has almost destroyed it. We were living in admittedly superficial harmony, but we were happy. We painted Easter eggs and decorated the Christmas tree, but that didn't make us Christians. I don't give a damn about the origin of these customs; most of them have pagan roots anyway. But they were family holidays. Our daughter loved them, and we were together, laughed together, ate together, and felt secure, or at least I thought so. But how am I suddenly to celebrate Passover? Or Sukkoth? I'd feel bizarre, like an Indian wearing Austrian national dress and yodeling. It doesn't suit me, because it isn't me. You must understand that.

ROBERT: I understand it. And I don't disagree as far as our daughter is concerned. I don't want to make her into a Jew, at any rate not as long as we're in Austria. Because to grow up

Jewish here is always connected with dark forebodings. We would have to prepare her to be always on guard, to recognize when it's time to get out. Perhaps it's better for her to become an ordinary Austrian, without divided loyalties and mixed feelings. You know that I often think of emigrating, even if for the time being I feel at home here, have my practice and make my living here. Still I'm haunted by the idea that I may be forced to leave. And in these flight fantasies I escape by myself. Whenever I think of leaving here I see myself alone in a train compartment, on a plane, perhaps with another man who also has had to flee. But never with a wife and a child. I always see the two of you staying here, surviving in safety as Austrians. Perhaps that's the real reason I am living with you rather than with a Jewish woman. To have to flee with a wife and child is the very worst thing imaginable. It may sound brutal and inhuman, but I don't want to have Jewish children.

And if they catch me? That's all right. Whether I live another few years or not doesn't matter. But my daughter? I can't even think of that. When I do, I see pictures of children in concentration camps, and I have to stop, I feel as if my head is split in two. You must do everything to save yourself and our daughter. Deny that I'm her father, accuse me of whatever you want, only save yourself and our daughter. My disappearance would in any case be a relief for you two.

ERIKA: That's some future you're painting for us. You're thinking of running away, and I'm to prepare myself not only to live without you but also to deny you as my daughter's father. But where do these fears of yours come from? You've never experienced persecution. You've grown up here like everybody else. Have you ever experienced hostility against Jews? You yourself have often said how friendly and courteous people were to you and that you never had any problems. Who here has ever

I Don't Share Your Yearning

threatened you or insulted you? Why do you keep on dwelling on an imaginary persecution? Can you survive only when you feel rejected? In that case I have to disappoint you. You are not rejected here. On the contrary, you are one of the privileged, whether you like it or not. But for the past year now, as soon as we get together with other people, you immediately bring up the fact that you are a Jew. You confront them with it in the hope that they will trip over it. Don't you think there is anything else about you that others might find interesting?

Sure, you're a Jew. Nothing can change that. But who and what else are you? Have you suddenly put your Jewishness before everything else? You're my husband, my lover, the father of my daughter, a physician. Or are you perhaps a Jewish physician, my Jewish lover, always a Jew first and everything else second?

For the past year you've been withdrawing from me. The more your past catches up with you, the more you retreat into it. More and more your Jewishness is becoming a second reality alongside your family. You're not the same Robert I once knew, the one I met almost six years ago. I have almost no contact with the new Robert. I feel excluded and deserted. Why don't you talk honestly with me about your feelings? I can't always talk to you only about the effects of Jewishness on you, I also have to know how it affects your feelings toward me. Do you stay with me only in order to lessen your fears of persecution? That's a fine basis for love.

ROBERT: I find that I'm less and less able to talk to you about it. You'll probably call it racism, but the only people with whom I can discuss my fantasies and ideas about Jewishness are Jews. Every conversation with non-Jews is like an interrogation. It turns into a pedantic discourse devoid of any notion of what's really going on in me. I have often experienced it, even, I'm sorry to say, when talking to you. You too are interested, curious, even fascinated by the stories of the past and the present, but you understand nothing. And at your first question I recoil, as though you'd slapped me in the face. Your questions, however well meant and full of genuine interest and compassion, often frighten me and show me how little you know me. True, you're horrified by the story of the extermination of my family, but you're also a little bit titillated. How often, when the topic of Jews has come up among friends, and even among strangers, have you described the death of my grandparents or my parents' life in the concentration camp, omitting no detail? It was like the evening news, a tidbit offered at a party or dinner, a little horror story to liven things up. You can't handle it, you are not a part of it, and you talk about it as though you knew more about it than anyone else. I was always so ashamed when that happened. It was like an account of a court hearing, a sensational news story, previously unknown and now made public for the first time. It was as though you were saying, look at whom I'm living with, you can't match that! Who were you supposed to shock with my stories? Above all, who with whom?

ERIKA: You've retreated into your defenses. Every non-Jew, even some Jews, are proof to you of a hostile or at least alien environment. They don't understand you; some even want to kill you. But you're making things easy for yourself with your contempt. Your cynicism has nothing to do with your Jewishness. Your feeling of strangeness here is not like that of an aborigine who suddenly finds himself in a strange civilization. Jews have always lived here in Austria, and they showed remarkable ability to adjust. That was the source of their strength. Your people were always able to begin all over again under the most difficult circumstances, regardless of whether they were observant or Orthodox or assimilated. If you took your origins seriously you would direct all your efforts toward finding a new home here. You'd do everything to gain a foothold here, to become one of the majority in this city, even if only one of the many Jews who are again living here, and make it possible for your family to live in peace and quiet. But you're doing exactly the opposite. You're destroying your family, and you despise the people here. What's so Jewish about that?

It frightens me to see how estranged we've become. And it wasn't like that before. We tried through our love and our daughter to show that reconciliation was possible, that we were not like our parents. Do you think it was easy for me to go with a Jew? My classmates, my girl friends, not to mention my family —I was always wondering whether to tell them or not. Was it something quite ordinary, not worth mentioning? Should I prepare them for it? Did I have to warn them against behaving awkwardly toward you? And then the reactions, above all when you weren't present. The desperately minimizing answers like, so what, a Jew, a person like any other, after all, times have changed. How hard they tried to deny the problems they were having with it. What support did you give me in those situations? When you were around you usually didn't say a word, and if you did, it was nothing but cynical remarks. How did you help me get through those painful situations? I am not a criminal, and neither are my friends. I am a child of the persecutors, just as you are a child of the victims. And if mastering the past is not a road you can take then we have no common road. Because I have to overcome the past, I must shake it off, must rid myself of the burden of tradition. But can I do it if you constantly keep reminding me of it, if I cannot help you solve it? In that case you deprive me of the chance to begin again, and with it also of the possibility of sharing a life with you. According to your logic you can live only with Jews and I only with non-Jews, preferably with the son of an SS officer. Together with him I should then try to atone and do penance.

Vienna happens to have an extremely anti-Semitic tradition, and neither you nor I will change it. The people here are malicious, stupid, and dangerous. I know it. If one lets them, they will continue to persecute and torture not only you but now also me and our daughter. What's at issue here is not a popular attitude that can change but the scope one allows them for their cruelty. But what does all that have to do with us?

ROBERT: Stop kidding yourself. You're not a victim here, not even if you're living with me. Of course I'm aware of how malicious the people here are, and I expect it. But that malice is directed at me, not at you or our daughter. If worse came to worst, you could go to your parents or to some other relatives. But I? If I fled to my parents I would only save them the trouble of transporting me separately; they'd have all of us in one fell swoop.

We're not getting anywhere. My return to religion, not only to tradition, is inevitable. And how that can be reconciled with my life with you concerns me greatly. We're no longer those carefree young people we were when we first met, who thought only of themselves. We're now thirty, have professions we like, and, I hope, are slowly growing up. In the early days of our love we shut everything out. There was something desperate, something exclusionary, about that hysterical need to be together all the time. We clung to each other like two drowning people in the hope of surviving together in a world that frightened us. Maybe I was the one who began to fear that I would drown together with you. Today I am drawn to the shores of my ancestors and intimates, to warmth and understanding and belonging. But why should that mean a separation from you? If we change, then our relationship also has to change.

I Don't Share Your Yearning

ERIKA: Your yearning is not my yearning. I've always dreamed of living as a free person with a free person. I can no more subordinate myself to a rabbi than I could to a Protestant clergyman. I want an independent man, guided but not enslaved by his beliefs. Whether we still have a joint road will depend on your journey into your world, into the world of your ancestors. And it is becoming intolerable for me to have to wait for your decision. I loved you before I knew that you were a Jew and I loved you when I found out. I saw in you, and I still do, a free person, not a prisoner on leave who is about to return to his cell. Where is that free will you used to be so proud of? Lately you've begun to assume the pose of a victim of circumstances. What happened to your free choice?

ROBERT: You're right, and then again you aren't. Fifty or sixty years ago it would have been my free choice. Judaism, Jewishness, to live within or outside the tradition, as a religious or assimilated Jew, against one's parents or with them, all that was possible. But Auschwitz changed all that. Since the Holocaust there has been no such thing as free choice. Now I can only react. I am following the lead of the dead and letting myself be guided by the fantasies they produce in me. My free will has turned into manipulated action, into an impediment, into a burden that makes it difficult for me to move freely. I am like a marionette that one can manipulate by pulling a string attached to its arms and legs. But attached to that string is the weight of 6 million murdered Jews. And you want me to be a free man?

9

Martha

I Wanted to Get Out of History

I AM twenty-eight years old, a journalist by profession. Also I am Jewish. I make a habit of telling this to anyone who wants to hear it as well as to anyone who doesn't. I know this sounds terribly confident and aggressive, but that wasn't always so. I think it wasn't till I was about twenty that I was able to speak about it openly. Before that I was very much under my parents' influence. They are completely different. They don't want anybody to know they're Jewish, and they act accordingly.

"It isn't all that important, you're better off keeping it to yourself so you won't run into any problems," they used to tell me. When I was around fifteen or sixteen I asked them whether they were afraid of living here in Vienna, and whether they had ever thought of emigrating. They indignantly denied it. "What are you talking about," they said, "this is a free country, a good country. What happened here once can never happen again. Just look at the world around you, unrest and catastrophes everywhere except here. Here it's peaceful." Never a word that the only reason they returned to Austria was the money, the restitution payments. Giving presents to the dead doesn't make any sense, but to pay the survivors for coming back not only makes more sense but also acts as a sop to the conscience. My parents now lead a quiet life, grateful for every day they can spend on this earth. I don't condemn them; I don't even criticize them for it. They've suffered so much in their lifetime that I have to admire and even love them for still being capable of carrying on.

Both survived a concentration camp. My father spent four years there, my mother three. They met after liberation in a convalescent home. And when they are asked how it is possible to live a completely normal life after all that horror, they smile serenely and say that it was a valuable experience and that they would not appreciate each day so fully had it not been for the camp. Their gentleness and humility made them seem invincible. Me rebel against them like other children of the sixties? Unthinkable!

I am very different. I have always told myself: not me. You won't break me or wipe your dirty shoes on my back.

My parents are very dear, sweet, and nice, so nice that one would never think of looking behind the façade. But behind that façade they are trembling, shaking from head to toe. They lead the life of a rabbit terrified by a snake. They're sitting at a bountiful table and now and then forget about the snake lying in wait. But it's there and they know it. Even when I was little I was struck by my parents' all-encompassing fear—of my teachers, of policemen, of a registered letter.

But my parents are not only mentally crippled. They are physically crippled as well. My father's feet, for example, are different sizes. He was fourteen when he came to the camp, a short, slender, tough child. They put him to work shoveling lime on the corpses in the mass graves. He was always standing with one foot in the lime, and it became stunted. My mother has two fingers missing on her left hand. She was put to work in a factory. Safety devices were probably not too common at the time, and certainly not in the case of prisoners. If one died another one was always available. On the other hand my mother's injury saved her life. An employee at the factory brought her to a doctor, who bandaged the hand. The accident happened shortly before the liberation, and in the general chaos during the final weeks in the camp she was able to hide.

At any rate, both of them survived. They were brought to a convalescent home, and there they met and fell in love. The time in that sanatorium is one of the most vivid pictures I have of my parents. They have repeatedly described their life there, unlike their time in the camp. That they can't talk about. When they first met after the war their heads were shaved and they were emaciated. The clothes they were given didn't fit; both of them, particularly my father, were emotional wrecks. During those first weeks in the clinic he kept on stealing bread and hiding it under the mattress. Even when it got moldy and the nurses wanted to throw it out he refused to give it up and would become hysterical. He couldn't believe that it was all over. Even today he can't get himself to throw away a piece of bread. So these two people, starved for love and affection, met in that home. To this day my parents have a very loving relationship. They are always together, are completely dependent on each other, and don't want to spend a minute apart. How puny what now passes for love seems to me, this desperate dressing up for an evening in the hope of meeting Mr. Right. I don't think I'll ever get married. The intensity and love that I saw at home don't exist any more.

I've had many affairs, with both Jews and non-Jews. But I

I Wanted to Get Out of History

always end up asking myself whether it's the same as it was for my parents when they met, whether I'm not perhaps blinded by appearance, by a name, a degree, a profession, a car, money, success. What would there be to that man, I ask myself, if he were in a camp, or if he were to see me in rags, filthy, with drooping breasts, skin and bones instead of my nicely rounded backside. I've also tried non-Jews. Even then my parents didn't object. Always those brief, well-meant words like, It's your life and you have to decide, but if you want our advice, marry a Jew.

I wanted to get out of history. I didn't want every circumcised penis to remind me of my murdered relatives. I wanted to handle love free of the burden of the past. My friends were Austrians, Italians, Frenchmen, whatever—but no Jews. Generally everything went along fine until they found out that I was Jewish, a Jewish woman living in Austria. Then came the fascination with the exotic, particularly in the case of Viennese men. For Viennese intellectuals a Jewish woman is as exotic as a Thai woman would be for the average worker. There's that titillating sensation of being in bed with someone forbidden, doing something for which you would have been arrested forty years ago. They suddenly became so kind, so understanding, as though I were handicapped. The difference between leftists and rightists was also interesting. There were those unpleasant leftist types who manifested their solidarity with the victims by making themselves out to be victims. I am on your side because I, a man of the Left, was persecuted by the Nazis just like you, and that sort of idiocy. Or the right-wingers, who told me how wonderful it was the way we're handling the Arabs. Then there were those with psychological insight. You poor child, all these psychic problems because of what happened to your parents, and so on. They wanted to turn me into a patient. Not one of them would simply accept me as a woman. I was the personification of their own problems with Jews. They gave me books about the persecution of the Jews under the Nazis, we went to movies about the persecution of the Jews, we discussed neo-Nazism and the politics of Israel. I became the dumping ground for their limited imagination, their insensitivity, their troubled relationship with the past.

When none of this worked out I tried it with Jews. At first it was simpler and more familiar, but it led to a very different set of problems. Most of them immediately wanted to bring me to their mothers, introduce me into the family, and after a week or two the two sets of parents would be introduced to each other. It turned into a big deal, and at first indirectly and then directly the topic of marriage would come up.

Of course I understand it. There are so few Jews here in Vienna, and the older people in particular are happy if their son or daughter manages to find one. But my original fear was confirmed. Every one of these young Jews was linked to some slaughtered innocents. There wasn't one of them who hadn't lost a family member during the war. If the non-Jewish Viennese men often lacked warmth and yearning, many of the young Jews were emotionally burned out, dead. Either driven, restless types, chasing after assimilation, thinking that a BMW or Mercedes and a hefty bank account made them into real Viennese, or those others forever whining that they were living in the wrong place among the wrong people—either left-wing softies dreaming of a Jewish patriarch or Jewish machos with blonde girl friends. "Look at me, the lousy Jew—I not only survived, but now I'm also taking your women away from you." I don't think I'll ever marry!

Last week I was invited to a wedding. He a Jew, a doctor, looking like a *Stürmer* caricature—short, stoop-shouldered, glasses, black hair, big nose, thick lips; she the daughter of an old

I Wanted to Get Out of History

Nazi—slim, tough, athletic, a head taller than he and a few years older. At first he wanted her to convert, but she refused. So they had a civil wedding. They wanted to have as many people as possible at the reception. But who? The wedding was neither Jewish nor Christian. They celebrated it in a summer cottage, invited hundreds of people, mostly acquaintances from work and neighbors. They all came, especially the neighbors. Someone in native Austrian dress made a speech. There stood the little Jew next to his Teutonic bride, while an unpleasant petty bourgeois in contemporary Nazilook delivered a humorous nuptial address. There was dancing, laughter, and boozing. And they behaved like they always do when they're having real fun. On the fringes of the garden a few lost people were standing around not knowing what to do with themselves. They were the handful of Jews who had come. Clumsy and helpless, they walked around and tried to make polite conversation. Inside everyone was dancing around the little Jew. Maybe he'll never understand it and maybe he doesn't want to, but whatever he does, he'll always be a little Jew. The dancing around him turned into a ritual act. His wife had refused to convert, so he was being converted. They wanted to pluck him out, like a piece of fruit, to sever him from his roots. And to all appearances they were succeeding.

Only time will tell how far he is willing to go to bury his past. Assimilation is an understandable act after all that has happened to us Jews. But total assimilation can turn into a betrayal of the dead. There can and must be forgiveness, otherwise it would be impossible to live in Vienna as a Jew. But not forgetting. And if today some of us dance with old or new Nazis, even if they're not wearing swastika armbands, it means that not only have the dead been incinerated but that they've also been forgotten. In one of his stories Georg Tabori has written something that I find very significant: One should be careful about looking the enemy in the eye lest one stop hating him.

We young Jews here in Vienna cannot simply mingle with the people as though nothing had happened. Above all we can't do that because our parents have stopped calling for revenge and for expiation by the criminals. All these major and minor vengeance campaigns of the Israelis against the Arabs are ridiculous and perverse. Nothing has been done against the real murderers, the Germans and Austrians. No vengeance, no retribution, not even rage; at most despair and mourning. Only the Eichmann trial—one of the few Austrians who at least was sentenced to death. But what else? Nothing. We, the victims, wanted money. Compensation for the gas we had to breathe in, for the flames that consumed us. If we had killed them in vengeance, who would then be left to make restitution?

And every time one of these filthy Nazis was freed we protested, and with us the liberal and left-wing intellectuals. Some writer would draft an indignant appeal and they all signed, and in this way they got their names in the paper. And the journal of the Jewish Community and a few progressive papers would publish it. Stylistically impeccable, beautifully formulated protests were issued, and perhaps one day they will find their way into anthologies of political essays. But nobody lay in wait for that exonerated swine, ready to kill him. He went home, embraced his wife, and that was that, and he probably also threw a little party for his friends to celebrate his victory.

Why doesn't anyone in this country kill out of mourning, indignation, or despair? Why only when ordered and backed by a regulation? What happened here in Austria and Germany after 1945 gives future murderers *carte blanche*. In future it will be permissible to murder here with a clear conscience if it doesn't violate accepted practices or decrees.

I Wanted to Get Out of History

And still, or more precisely because of this, I live here in Vienna. All these tensions, this rage of mine, are a source of energy and form the basis of my writing. Sometimes a day doesn't pass that I don't have a fight with someone, whether a taxidriver or the grocer. When I sense the smallest sign of Nazism, anti-Semitism, or hostility toward foreigners, I fight with them, yell, call them names. My journalism also deals mainly with these themes. Not that I expect to change people, but I don't want to make it too easy for them. I want them to know that there is someone who isn't afraid to yell loudly when she hears that crap.

I have also tried living in Israel. I'd gone there after finishing college. Before I went I used to say that Israel meant nothing to me, that I was a Jew, not an Israeli. But when I stood in front of the Wailing Wall for the first time, I broke into tears. I collapsed and was completely annihilated. I still can't talk about it, but it was the most intense experience of my life. I spent an entire year in Israel. It turned out to be a great disappointment, but still it was an important experience. Ultimately I had to recognize that it wasn't the same country my parents and my friends had been telling me about. It wasn't the country in which Jews treat each other as if they were happy finally to be among themselves. And my notions about the chosen people in the land of Israel were also disappointed. It's a country like any other, with thieves, robbers, murderers, and prostitutes. When I was little I couldn't imagine that Jews could also be evil. Only the others who took everything away from us Jews and killed us could be bad. So if there were no others, then there couldn't be any bad ones. Childish logic. The reality was very different, not only for me but also for many other European Jews.

When I returned to Vienna from Israel, I was offered a very interesting job at a major periodical. Here, too, I had experiences involving my naïveté about Jews. One of my colleagues, a Jew, was very friendly and nice and I trusted him completely. Later I found out that he had intrigued against me when I tried to get a promotion that would have made me his boss. It was a real shock to me. I was terribly upset, mostly about my own gullibility. Why had I trusted him blindly? Just because he was circumcised?

We Jews in Vienna have nobody, not even the other Jews. The table at which we sit is not our own, and we gulp down our bread before somebody comes along and takes it away from us. Our life is like a respite from prison. Those who survived are now allowed to get a whiff of freedom, but any day we could be ordered back into our cells. Maybe that's the reason we live so intensely and tend to exaggerate things. The small Jewish shopkeeper is as relentless in his drive to succeed as the physician who gets to be a professor more quickly than any of his colleagues. We are creating a new hatred of Jews because the few of us who are living in Vienna are extraordinarily industrious and successful. But the others don't understand us. They don't want to understand that we don't have as much time as they do. Because the time will come when someone will again decide to take everything away from us and kill us all. And everybody will join in again, above all here in Vienna. The cruelty of the Austrian people is a fact for me. From the stories of my parents and their friends I learned that the people here behaved much worse toward the Jews than the people in Germany.

What is important for us Jews is life here on earth. We don't believe in hell or paradise. And such ridiculous figures as the devil of the Christians don't frighten us. All that goyish stuff with angels and trumpets and welcoming committees at the Pearly Gates. We have to wait until Judgment Day, until the Messiah comes. And until then we will lie in our wooden boxes. We Jews

I Wanted to Get Out of History

have a very different relationship to our God than the Christians do. Why should God let us live better after death than before? What reason could He have?

But since the Nazis everything has changed. One can't make contracts with a God of vengeance. I believe that for us Jews World War II was like the Deluge. They all went into the gas ovens. My pious grandparents here and the less pious ones there. Maybe they were grasping and tried to cheat the peasant to whom they sold a pair of pants. Or maybe not, I don't know. But the old Jew who spent all day in prayer at the synagogue, on Yom Kippur and every other day, also went into the gas chamber, the one who never spent a moment alone in a room with a woman, who turned away when a strange woman spoke to him because he didn't want to live immodestly, not even in his thoughts. He, too, went into the gas chamber. All were caught. No amount of piety could save anyone from death.

My parents brought me up to be very religious. We went to synagogue regularly. But when I began to think for myself, I began to doubt the existence of God. And if there is a God, then He has allowed evil to seep into the world. The good are dying out. The person I admire most is Egon Friedell. When the Gestapo came to get him, he opened his third-floor window and called down, "Be careful! Take cover!" And then he jumped. Such consideration, such sensitivity. He was a nondescript, fat man of enormous humanity. Those times are over and gone. Stefan Zweig with his reveries about the hundred years before the Nazis, his fantasies about democracy and culture, his passionate desire for assimilation—all that is gone, stamped out by the boots of the Nazis.

Perhaps we are a people doomed to extinction. From the time of the Jewish war against the Romans up to the founding of the state of Israel, Jews had not engaged in warfare. The trade of war was the most despised one, the most stupid thing one could engage in. The second most stupid occupation was trading. The only thing thought worthwhile was the study of the Bible. How can such a people survive among barbarians?

As a child in school I was fascinated by stories of the Crusades and the brave knights and beautiful damsels. I drew pictures of their costumes and imagined I was one of the beautiful princesses waiting for her prince. But somewhere in these tales about the Crusades I came across a little sentence, insignificant and unnoticed by all the others, saying that the brave knights while passing through some city or other killed all the Jews. Well, that was the end of the princess for me. Again I was on the other side, on the side of the vanquished.

Yet despite everything I believe that somehow I am happy. I love my work, my colleagues take me seriously, and I have found a boyfriend, a non-Jew, who allows me to breathe freely but who also lets me live as a Jew with all my rituals. And if a new dictatorship should come that kills us Jews then I'll die, maybe a few years before my time. But fear? Fear no longer exists since the tragedy of my parents' generation. Because atomic war is the next Deluge. And that one won't spare anyone, not even those who unleash it.

10

Aryeh

A Life Like Any Other

I WAS BORN in 1948 in Israel, my mother's first and only son. It wasn't until I was nine years old that my parents went to Germany. I was still in Israel during the 1956 war. The bombing of Tel Aviv, the ruins, the screams of the people, and everywhere the tears of the parents whose sons had been killed—I still remember all that. It is something I will never forget. My brother—he is much older than I, the child of my father's first marriage—was a high-ranking army officer, and we lived in constant fear for his life.

One day, I remember it as if it were today, I was sitting on the stoop of the bunker during an air raid and told myself that my brother would come back the next day. Everybody laughed at me. It was war, and a soldier couldn't just come and visit his family. But the next day he arrived, just stood there in the doorway with a case of Coca-Cola. It was like a treasure. We'd heard a lot about it but had never tasted it. The case was stowed away carefully and we were each given only one bottle a week. Ever since then I have believed in premonitions, and I also take my dreams seriously.

But despite all the troubles during the war nothing terrible happened to us. Nobody was wounded, and our house wasn't hit. Still it was an important event, and it affected the life of my parents. They'd simply had enough. Enough of war, enough of the fear that their sons could be killed in a war, of taking shelter during air raids, and so on. All they now wanted was to live in peace.

My father, a physician, initially wanted to go to Switzerland, but there he would have had to take licensing exams. He was already more than fifty and didn't want to do that, and so we went to Germany.

For my father it was a return. He came from Germany, and I think he was even happy to be here again. Basically he had always remained a German, spoke German at home, and in all the years in Israel he never learned to speak Hebrew properly. Even when I visualize him today—he's been dead almost ten years—I see him as a German. He looked like one, and he felt like one. He was completely out of place among the Orientals in Israel. But for my mother and myself Germany at that time was an alien, hostile land. For us it was anything but a homecoming. I was young and somehow able to adjust to things, but my mother never really fitted in here. She was a beautiful woman given to sadness, but here in Germany she grew increasingly more silent and depressive. The only way she could live here was with my father by her side. When he died, her will to live also died. A few weeks later she voluntarily joined him in death. And here I was in a country that had never been home and never will be, deserted by my parents, by a mother for whom I

A Life Like Any Other

was never reason enough to go on living. My half-brother had long since gone to Canada, and I was not in touch with him.

My father originally left Germany in 1933. He went to Palestine. The English admitted him because he was a doctor. Many members of his family were able to escape in time and are now scattered throughout the world. While he was alive I still had the feeling that there was such a thing as a large family. We were always entertaining some visiting uncle or cousins. With him I was able to rid myself of the feeling that there was no one left anymore. But even in his case there was tragedy. His parents remained behind because they had taken in a sick cousin. When they were at the point of joining my father, it was already too late. Both his parents and his cousin were killed.

My links to my father are still very strong. He was a tall, proud man, a real patriarch. The family was always the most important thing for him. Relatives kept visiting us from all over the world; he was the head of the scattered family, whether they were living in Israel, Germany, or South America.

We had a huge apartment here in Germany. In it my parents conducted both their private and their business lives. There my father had his office, my mother her little dressmaking business, and in the rest of the rooms we ate, slept, received company— there was nothing we lacked. It was like in the old shtetl where everything was under one roof. There was no strict division between business hours and leisure time. Work was just as much a part of life as anything else. In theory it was possible for a patient waiting for his appointment to be measured for a new pair of pants and afterward have dinner with the family.

Meals were important events in our house. My father was a specialist in Western cuisine, my mother in Eastern cooking. Every meal was a ceremony, a little feast. When I look back, those days with my parents were a lovely time. It was a real home. I haven't managed to duplicate it with my own family. After my mother joined my father in death ten years ago I was numb. I mourned them for seven years. I was barely able to work, wandered around here and there, found no place in which I could live, no friends that interested me. That period is lost to me, I have hardly any memories of it. Seven years of suspended animation. Now I'm slowly trying to regain my balance.

I couldn't forgive my mother for deserting me. She had never felt comfortable here in Germany. She was afraid of everything, always afraid. My father was her only protection. My relationship with her was always problematic, but in the final analysis what happened under the Nazis was responsible for it.

She came from the East, from a small village in Galicia. Her family had moved there from Austria, and in that little village they belonged to the elite. Her father had his own lumber business, German was spoken at home, and though they were never really integrated into the life there they were accepted. Perhaps I am romanticizing my mother's family, but when I read books like Joseph Roth's *Job* I think that's how things must have been there. At the same time these images depress me, above all when I see pictures of the old Galicia and read about the harmony that existed there despite all differences, where outsiders were just as important as the rabbi. How impoverished and ludicrous is the life of the Jews here in Germany by comparison. All the money we got after the war couldn't bring the dead back to life, nor were we able to restore the warmth, the human contact of the past. I can't even think about all that, it depresses me even more than thinking about the dead.

My mother left Poland for Israel very early, I think in 1934, under the auspices of a Zionist organization. It turned out to be both her good fortune and her misfortune. She was saved, but

A Life Like Any Other

her entire family—eight brothers and sisters, her parents, and all her relatives—stayed behind and were slaughtered. Yes, slaughtered! I insist on these terms, slaughtered and murdered. I get furious whenever I hear that so and so many Jews from this or that city died. What do you mean died? Germans died during the bombings or during the liberation by the Allies. But my family was murdered, with premeditation and bureaucratic planning. Their murder was neither coincidence nor accident nor the unauthorized act of some fanatical Nazi or savage criminal. It was the small, nasty Herr Mueller and Herr Maier who every day, putting on their freshly laundered white shirts, pressed pants, and swastika lapel pins, went to their offices, sat down at their desks, and checked off the names on the list of Jews of the town that were to be taken away.

When I now have to go to a government office in Germany I see them sitting there, these lickspittles, these ass-crawlers. Biermann is right with his song about functionaries. If in 1945 the Allies had really wanted to clean up Germany they should have sewn up the assholes of the Nazis they sentenced to death . . . Sometimes when I come across an official old enough to have been there I get the urge simply to hit out. Perhaps he's even sitting in the same room and is checking off the names of the Turks who're to be deported.

As to my mother, they not only took away her family, they also destroyed her life. For her to go on living as the only one left was more than she could bear. When the few survivors surfaced after the war she waited for news day in, day out, week in, week out—yes, year in, year out—hoping against hope that perhaps one of her relatives might turn up. Maybe it was coincidence and maybe not—some say there is no such thing as coincidence —but when my mother was carrying me she learned that no member of her immediate family, neither her sisters nor her parents, had survived. What she then wanted more than anything was a daughter, maybe in memory of her many sisters. Instead she got a son, a son who was unwanted and unloved, at least at first.

I am only now beginning to understand how greatly her disappointment has affected me and my life. When I was little she treated me like a girl. I was always neatly dressed, wasn't allowed to dirty myself or act like a typical boy. That's probably why I became gay. I am not about to offer any profound psychological interpretations, but I can see at least a connection between my homophile bent and my relationship to my mother. I was her only child, and I was the wrong one. I was supposed to resurrect the dead and I refused, denied her the possibility of solace and forgiveness.

I am now trying to become reconciled with my mother, mostly through my painting. I painted her as she lay dying, and that has helped me forget my resentment of her. She deserted me! Who do I still have today? She turned and left me. I wasn't worth living for. Without my father she didn't want to live. And I was neither the wished-for daughter nor the strong son who could replace the father. I didn't have a family, I didn't give her a daughter-in-law, and I didn't give her grandchildren. What was the use of living in such a world?

For me her death was a punishment, the final, ultimate punishment. She had always said that she'd have to starve once my father was gone. That fear was always with her, and with the passage of time it grew. Perhaps suicide is the final consequence if one is the sole survivor and constantly has to live with the question of why the others, why not me.

All these thoughts that I now ascribe to my mother also occupy me, and at times I don't know whether they are actual memories or my imagination. What is the point of living? A homosexual, a gay Jew. I once read that Rabbi Eliezer said that whoever is not concerned with being fruitful and multiplying acts as though he were shedding blood.

I soon began to realize that with my feelings I was even more of an oddity among Jews than among the goyim. Only rarely did I have affairs with Jews, but I have always dreamed of it. To live together with a Jew, to celebrate the holidays, to go to the synagogue, to sing, to read the Scriptures together, to find a substitute for the lost family. But it generally didn't work with Jews. It was as if even more than the non-Jews we had to be ashamed of our feelings. With non-Jews it was always much simpler, but somehow without feeling and unromantic. Love for a Jewish man will probably remain an unfulfilled dream.

But in other areas as well, Judaism, or rather my Jewishness, is increasingly becoming the basis of my identity. In my painting, for example, I deal primarily with Jewish themes. Buber and Chagall have influenced me greatly.

There were times when this aspect didn't touch me very much, but it was always there, always a part of me, even during my revolutionary period in the early seventies, when we went around proclaiming that Israel meant nothing to us. When we opened the newspaper the first question always was, "What does it say about Israel?"

For some years I've toyed with the idea of emigrating to Israel, but I haven't done it. Perhaps it's enough for me to feel that I can go, that there's a country to which I can escape anytime I want. The desperation of the Jews in the Third Reich, not knowing where to go, and the constant fear of being turned away; at least I'll be spared that the "next time."

Some years ago there was a fire in my building. Firemen came, there was a big fuss, tenants ran out on the street. That's when I became fascinated with the idea of fleeing. Thoughts about what to do if I suddenly had to flee went through my mind. What would I take along? Would I remain calm or go to pieces? Would I be up to the demands of the situation? Or would I give myself up?

The way I would handle such an escape has been preoccupying me for years. What bothers me is not so much the fear of having to flee, but rather the fear that I wouldn't manage it well enough. I've never had to run away, have no experience in that area. I grew up sheltered, looked after, cared for. Perhaps if push came to shove I'd be too cowardly.

Recently I found an old steamer trunk in a junk shop. It opens up like a wardrobe, with drawers on one side. At least once a week I pack this trunk in my imagination, taking along things that at that moment seem the most important to me.

Last week, for example, my paintings seemed most important. You've got to take them along, I thought to myself, everything else can be replaced. But then I thought that they'd be too heavy. I'd have to be able to lift the trunk. This imaginary flight also represents the most extreme form of loneliness. One cannot and must not rely on anyone, everyone is a potential enemy, however supportive he may appear. And loneliness is the most important and most difficult thing we Jews here in Germany must learn to deal with. I have firsthand experience with so-called friends, non-Jews who make a point of stressing how liberal they are and how repugnant anti-Semitism is to them, but who become insulting, crude, and malicious at the slightest disagreement. A friend of mine who is completely non-Jewish in appearance once went into business with a goy. For a while everything went smoothly and his partner never gave any sign of prejudice. But after some years their business failed, and then it began: "I should have known, one can't have any dealings with Jews." Perhaps this is typically German, this blind, uncontrolled rage when faced with failure or pressure. In school we were told that the mass unemployment in the 1930s was the reason the people were so easily misled. I asked myself, What has that to do with my grandfather? Just because they were out of work, did they have to slaughter him and my grandmother, my aunts and uncles? Did that make it better for them? Did it make it easier for them to bear their lot? I don't understand why supposedly intelligent people lend themselves to disseminating such drivel in the schools.

In 1957, when I came to Germany and went to school here, I met with the most varied reactions. On the one hand some kids spat at me and called me names, while on the other hand the teachers treated me so gingerly that I'd have to say I had it a little easier than the rest. That of course didn't endear me to my classmates. But despite all the difficulties, the few Jews at our school were always in the forefront of things. Once—I think it was in the sixth or seventh grade—we were six Jews in our class. It was almost like being a majority. Also, my Jewish classmates always wanted to be the best. I was never very good in school, but they knew everything and mastered everything, as though they had a mission to succeed. Although I was glad to have the protection of this powerful group, their ambition got on my nerves. As an Israeli I also considered the Jews here extremely German. I found these hard-working, decent, upright, assimilated German Jews more German than Jewish.

Incidentally, at that time I never went to the German synagogue but to the American temple. There were other reasons for that as well. The atmosphere there was entirely different. The people there hadn't experienced persecution and hadn't had to leave their homes. It was the temple of the victors, not an assemblage of victims. But there were other, formal differences. Nobody paid any attention to dress or other superficial things.

With the Germans I always had the feeling that I had to dress properly, and so on. I sometimes ask myself whether my prejudice against Germans doesn't extend to the German Jews. I feel most comfortable with people who are both foreigners and Jews, or at least who have grown up abroad.

As a teenager I went to the same discotheque as most of the other Jews. Non-Jews also went there, girls in particular, but they were exploited. They became very unsure and embarrassed, like outsiders among exotic, colorful birds.

On the whole my life in Germany as a teenager was no different from anybody else's. I never really had the feeling of being discriminated against and never ran into any particular difficulties. I wouldn't want to overstate the problems I faced as a Jew. I was a carefree youngster who really didn't let the things that had happened spoil his life. Of course there was anger against people who had played an active role under the Nazis. But on the other hand there was also the exaggerated circumspection and politeness of my teachers, and later of my bosses.

When I went to work in a bank instead of taking my final high-school exams, the other trainees even appointed me their spokesman. I never kowtowed to my superiors and was not afraid to speak up. Whatever demands I made were granted. We didn't want to wear dark suits and asked for a longer lunch break and more frequent rotation among the various departments. The others were afraid to speak up and always sent me. I got everything we asked for. It was almost grotesque how extremely polite and friendly they were toward me, whatever the demand.

But one day I decided I'd had enough of all this. I was twenty-one, and the hypocritical friendliness and the way I was being used by my fellow workers because I was Jewish became repugnant. I had become a clown, a terminally ill patient whose every wish was granted in the few weeks left to him.

A Life Like Any Other

I packed all my belongings, including my furniture, into a huge shipping container and went to Canada. Earlier I had applied for emigration. I wanted to leave Germany for good. Then I took my final exams and began to study. That was when I discovered my aptitude for graphic art and painting.

The more I worked in art, the stronger grew my interest in becoming more involved in Judaism—*my* kind of Judaism. It wasn't so much a question of *the* Jewish problem, but more and more the question of my identity, roots, and affiliation. And when I returned to Germany on my vacation I felt that as far as I was concerned this search for roots was possible only here in Germany. I am the son of a German Jew, and the story of my parents is also my story. By running away I would also be running away from my own past. I realized that as a German Jew I needed the German setting and above all the contact with other German Jews, to stimulate my creativity and imagination.

In Canada, for example, I had hardly any contact with the Jewish community, and the majority of my friends were non-Jews. Here in Germany it is different. It seems odd, but in the meantime I've begun to feel almost at home here. My European vacation became a return to Germany, the second one in my life, but the first one based on my own free choice, paralleling my father's decision. In order to rediscover the role of the stranger, I had to experience that feeling here.

I have now been living in Germany again for more than ten years, in a country where I get upset when I see signs like "German butter" or "German Red Cross." But I'm slowly beginning to understand that as far as other Jews are concerned, I am a German. When I went to Florence for Easter this year I wanted to go to the synagogue. They didn't let me in. They barred me. At first I was shaken, but then I thought, my expectation of Jews, this expectation of community, it's all an illusion.

As far as the Italians were concerned I was just another German, someone they'd rather not have among them. And here in Germany I can also see that even though there are only a few Jews, there are enormous differences among them. It bothers me to hear that a majority vote for the CDU. But then my father was an officer in the Prussian army, as was his father before him. Sometimes I wonder what would have happened if the Nazis had not been so anti-Semitic. How many Jews would have gone along with them?

Today I am living in Germany—a homosexual, a Jew, and a leftist. It is almost like the joke I heard about a Black in the New York subway who is reading a Yiddish Communist paper. Another passenger asks, "Isn't being black enough for you?"

I am trying to establish myself here in Germany with my art. Until recently I worked in a youth center, but I gave it up. Even there they wrote things against me on the wall. It's a blow to come into a place where you think you are doing a good job and are at least halfway accepted to find graffiti like "Jewish swine." I was able to talk to the young people about it, but the director lost her head. She scurried around with a red face trying to clean it all off. It embarrassed her, like pornographic drawings on the walls of a parochial school. But she didn't see any point in talking it over with the kids.

The rejection and hatred of Jews will always be part of my life. I cannot escape it or cast it off like old clothes. But does that make my life particularly interesting? I don't think so. It's a life like any other.

11

Edith

We the Living Dead of This Land

MY FATHER returned to Germany as a victor, in American army uniform. When he left Germany in 1938, the only one of his family to get out, he was one of the vanquished, driven out, humiliated. He ran for his life, and he escaped capture by the SS only because a German policeman tipped him off. He came to the United States via Switzerland, France, and Portugal. When he got there he wanted to enlist in the army to fight the Germans. At first he was rejected, but finally he was able to enlist and ultimately helped defeat the enemy.

For me my father's story holds great significance. He didn't come back here because he pined for Germany, an imaginary homeland, or because he couldn't wait to collect restitution. The reason he returned was to strike at those who had savaged him and his relatives.

Even now when he talks about his early days in the United States after escaping from Germany, his rage is still tangible.

The idea of revenge was uppermost in his mind. He landed in Sicily with the American army, and step by step he approached his former homeland, until one day he crossed the German border. According to him, that was one of the most important moments in his life. Yet it was also an enormous disappointment. He wasn't the welcome liberator, wasn't cheered as in Italy, where the people were happy to be rid of the Germans. The Germans didn't thank him for his help in delivering them from the Nazis. On the contrary, he was often accused of being a traitor and collaborator.

Years later I heard these things, too—in shops, school, apparently casual, off-hand remarks, often completely out of context. "Your father," they'd say, "well, he fought with the others, against us; of course, that was very brave of him, I've got to admit, but . . ."

Always that "but," this "against us." By "we" they meant the German army, their own fathers and sons. And perhaps my father had killed one of them, maybe the baker's husband or son. That he had liberated them from a dictatorship was never mentioned; never a word of praise or admiration, never did a teacher tell us that not all German men were either German soldiers or victims of fascism.

For example, I once suggested that my history teacher invite my father to talk to the class about his experiences, about a life that was very different from that of most others. But I got only evasive answers, that in that case others from the other side would also have to be invited. As though it were a matter of different, conflicting opinions.

After the war my father stayed in Germany. He left the army after two years, and ever since then he has lived here as a German, exactly as he did before the war. No, not exactly. He met my mother here. She had returned from a camp after being interned for three years. I know nothing about that period in my mother's life. She's never spoken about it, and nobody asks her. The little I've found out was accidental, from conversations I overheard with friends and relatives. I learned, for example, that she was transported together with her mother, that her mother died in camp, and that she herself survived only because she was such a fine musician. She played the violin even while in camp. But that's all I know about that time, and it's a good thing. I don't really want to know any details about the suffering and horror in the camp. It would only torture and weigh on me. That's why I've never asked my mother any questions. She survived that madness, overcame it, and despite it she retained all the faculties essential to a happy life. What happened to her seems just as unreal as Grimm's fairy tale about the six goats released from the belly of the wolf. I still don't go to movies about concentration camps, don't read any books about that time, and avoid all descriptions of survivors. I am grateful to my mother that she has spared me the details of her life in the camp.

I was born in 1950 to a Jewish family that observed all the rituals and customs. It was my parents' desire that I should preserve and continue the tradition. That's what they hoped for, but the reality unfortunately was different. I soon realized that in this land of restitution-payers the daughter of restitution-payees could not simply live as a Jew. Because despite my father's victorious entrance into Germany, despite my mother's resilience, they didn't live like people who had vanquished evil and now could live in peace.

I recently talked to my parents about it. I told them that I had grown up in an atmosphere of fear, that as a child I sensed their fear and behaved accordingly. The governing principle of our lives was to remain inconspicuous and not let anyone know that we were different. "I saw you as fearful," I told them. They were perplexed and hurt. "On the contrary," said my father, and he got very excited, "it was precisely the other way round. When I returned the others were very small and your mother and I were proud and brave. We wanted to help build a new Germany, a better one, where one could live in peace."

Maybe they felt that euphoria right after the war, but apparently it didn't last long, because they again were made to feel insignificant and fearful.

The story of my first day at school shows how helplessly I reacted to the matter of Jewishness. There we were, all the girls in neat dresses, and the teacher gave us some general rules of conduct, told us that we mustn't address her by the familiar *du*, and the like. And then, at the end, we were told to register for religious instruction. We waited on line, each child stating her religion—Roman Catholic, Protestant, Roman Catholic, Protestant, the only two mentioned. I stood way back and was completely confused. What were they talking about? I thought and I thought; when the teacher got to me, I didn't know what to say. No one else had said that she was Jewish, that word was never spoken, and I didn't know whether I was allowed to say it here. When I finally stood in front of the teacher, I began to stutter until I finally told her that I was nothing.

My mother went to the school, after I told her about it, and talked to the teacher. Even back then I was unable to say the word *Jew* or *Jewish* easily. As a matter of fact my parents even told me that I had done the right thing, that it wasn't necessary for the others to know. And today they are surprised when I tell them that I thought of them as fearful.

I didn't have the feeling of simply belonging to a different religious community. My otherness lacked a positive element, it was something better left unsaid, something one kept to oneself, but not because of any dramatic incidents involving anti-Semitism or anything like that. No, it was rather a quiet, hidden, but constant fear and uncertainty that something about me, and naturally also about my parents, wasn't quite right.

I was twelve when I accidentally found out that my mother had been in a concentration camp. I knew about the persecution of Jews, but more as a historical fact, not as a part of my parents' past. Or perhaps I was still too young to deduce the truth from casual remarks. But then, when I was around twelve, it suddenly became clear to me that we were the ones who were the subject of all that horror, that it was my mother who had experienced it herself, that it was my grandparents who were murdered by gas, were shoved into the cattle cars. All the cruelties that up to then I had only seen or heard about by chance suddenly involved me, my own family.

That created a strange emotion in me, hard to describe, like the icy gust of wind blowing through a flimsy hut I had read about in fairy tales. Suddenly many things became clear to me.

As I got older, my Jewish consciousness grew stronger and stronger. A trip to Israel at the age of fifteen was a turning point. There in Israel suddenly everybody was like my parents. The cadence of their speech, its music and rhythm, it was all familiar. Everything there seemed right, fell into place. When people got excited they gesticulated just like my parents. They laughed like my parents, they got annoyed like them, and I was a part of them, became submerged in a mass of similarities and patterns. It was a marvelous feeling.

Dozens of seemingly insignificant incidents strengthened my feeling of belonging not to a people scattered throughout the world, hiding in holes, but to a people moving freely here in Israel in large numbers. What fascinated me most of all was their disdain for authority. When I walked with my parents in parks with paths so narrow that signs were needed to indicate the direction, we followed the markers but hundreds of others didn't. If there was a fence and a notice saying that climbing the fence was forbidden, there was sure to be a hole to climb through right under the sign. Traffic signals, like all other rules, were a provocation. Everything and everybody was disputed, nothing was sacred or automatically accepted.

Israel was a milestone in my life. In my final years in high school the experiences connected to Jewishness became more and more concrete. Two things became clear to me. First of all I wasn't as alone as I had thought, even when I was the only Jew in a group, and second, I was different from the others and they would never understand me. When my classmates told Jewish jokes and tried to imitate Jewish speech, it sounded ridiculous. It had nothing to do with the language spoken by me or other Jews. And when they said to me the Jews are fantastic, they can turn anything into money and they stick together, that also had nothing to do with me. My parents always had money problems, and they had no close friends among the other Jews here. Nothing they said had anything to do with me, yet it was always directed at me.

When I was sixteen I joined a Jewish youth group, and the discussions there helped intensify my feeling of strangeness, of being misunderstood and surrounded by emotional zombies. My Jewish friends were the one thing I had to hang onto. We had very heated political debates, but emotionally we were coming from the same place.

After my graduation I traveled. I enjoyed moving around from place to place, a stranger everywhere yet without any memories of the past. In the Orient it didn't matter whether I was dark or light; to the native population I was just another stranger, someone from far away, rather than a stranger in my own country. It was a very pleasant feeling, a kind of security blanket in a totally alien environment. In Hong Kong the blond Swede with whom I traveled for a while was as much a stranger as I, the dark Jewish woman, never mind how he looked, how he talked, who his parents were, and whether he was circumcised or not. As far as the Chinese were concerned, both of us were equally strange.

When I returned I decided to go to college. I was twenty and fired up by the student movement. For a while I considered going abroad to study and getting away from Germany, but I couldn't do it. The German language was too important to me. I had a reading knowledge of Hebrew and English, but neither could equal my love for the German language. In English and in Hebrew I lacked the nuances, the ambiguities that make up a language. And so I went to Berlin, the mecca of the Left, to study.

Berlin, that was my dream, that's where I might still be able to learn something, find friends and people who shared my political leanings. I expected a radical change. I hoped to find Utopia, but instead I fell flat on my face. In 1972–73 everything in Berlin was in the hands of the Left. The student revolt was over, and leftist professors were everywhere. There was great flexibility, and I could choose any course or seminar I wanted. In that setting I hungrily fell on everything that was critical and revolutionary. The students also had a voice in the teaching of a course, and I found it very exciting; discussions and arguments in class were completely new to me. But I ran into open knives. In my naïveté I equated the Left with antifascism, and antifascism could never be anti-Semitic. However, the young left-wingers running around here were left because their parents were right. They knew nothing about anti-Semitism, let alone Judaism, nor did they have any sensitivity about it. The experiences I had here in my first years could fill a book. Again and again we read texts that were anti-Semitic, not subtly or obscurely but unambiguously, clumsily, stupidly anti-Semitic. And I'd sit there and wait for the others to become indignant, hoping that I wouldn't have to be the one to bring it up, for after all wasn't I among left-wing comrades-in-arms, new thinkers? But there was nothing, not a word. And there came a time when I couldn't control myself any longer and got excited and irritated and told them what was going on. Their reaction was embarrassed silence. They looked at me wide-eyed, and there were whispered remarks like, "She's supersensitive, a bit neurotic, can hear the grass grow, emotionally unstable," and so on.

If I had been a Vietnamese, they would have listened and perhaps have said, "Yes, maybe you're right, we never thought of it, we just don't know enough about it." But in my case it was neurosis. A psychically deformed victim. The child of victims suffering from a persecution complex can't be taken seriously, she is after all a victim herself.

The worst incidents are still with me. In a seminar on popular literature we read Konsalik's *Doctor from Stalingrad*. There we meet German prisoners of war—hard men, honest soldiers— and also decent Russians, a little primitive and barbaric perhaps, but decent and honest. Then comes a Russian woman doctor, a lusty, full-blooded Bolshevik woman, passionate, with flashing eyes, and a Russian male doctor who's also all right. And then we are introduced to yet another character—slit-eyed, with dirty hair, rejected by all. A slimy little rat. He is a Jewish interpreter. So, when we broke up into working groups, my group engaged in an interminable analysis and interpretation of the anti-Russian racism. But not a word about the Jew. And again I spoke up and asked whether nobody had noticed how the Jew was portrayed here. Embarrassed silence. They sat there saying nothing, but then came a long discussion about whether that point should be

We the Living Dead of This Land

included in our joint paper. And when the paper was read in the seminar, again nothing, not a word about it. Not a single one got up and said, "Oh my God, I didn't even notice it," or some such thing. Nothing! Only silence! They've learned nothing in these last years. They stupidly echo some handed-down phrases, above all when that makes them into leftists, so superior to their parents. But a feeling, a sensitivity for racism and anti-Semitism? No, nothing!

And so it went, in one seminar after another. One of the courses dealt with journalism in the Weimar Republic and the Soviet Union. Comparative contemporary history. I looked forward to that seminar. I thought of Egon Erwin Kisch and all the Jews of that period.

But when we read those articles nobody pointed out that most of them were written by Jews. And the ones we discussed in detail weren't. I remember one of them in particular, a piece of social criticism about Berlin by some count or other. He strolled through the city, saw a workers' demonstration being broken up by the police, wandered into the upper-class district where everybody was dressed in furs, then into the workers' quarter where the people were tubercular and pale, crowded together in small apartments with moldy walls, children in rags. And then he came to the Jewish quarter. There things got really bad. Everything was filthy, the children with scabies, the men with dirty *peyes*, standing around all day gesticulating. I read it and thought to myself, okay, my dear count, I know where you stand. Then came the professor's crucial question: "To judge by this article, would you say the count was left-wing or right-wing?"

I spoke up. He was a right-winger and an anti-Semite. But the others disagreed; they thought he was a leftist and a Communist. "Okay," I said, "in that case he was an anti-Semitic Communist;

127

they also existed." That really got them. How could I say such a thing, his imagery showed his unequivocal social involvement, he just happened to see those few Jews that way, that didn't make him an anti-Semite.

But I wouldn't let go. I asked them whether they didn't see that the workers, for example, were depicted very differently from the Jews. And I talked and talked, but nothing happened. Again only silence, until the professor spoke up and closed the discussion by telling us that the author was a man of the Left, and if that's how he described it that's how it must have been.

Period. That's it. The professor, incidentally, was a well-known leftist activist who signed his name to every appeal against injustice anywhere in the world. But as far as I was concerned he was blind and heartless, without any real feeling for the injustices he was trying to fight.

His statement left me speechless. That's not what I had in mind when I came to left-wing Berlin full of enthusiasm. I came here to participate in a new movement, to find a new approach to literature and history. But what I found instead was a repetition of my childhood experiences raised to the academic and intellectual plane. That's not what I had expected.

And there was one incident after another. It was like a didactic play about the New Wave in Germany. The young generation, the New Left, so proud of their new consciousness, were reenacting the past under new symbols. They were thrilled by the angry reactions of their parents. Like the little boy who says "shit" in front of his father for the first time, that's how the terminology of the Left poured out of their mouths. But nothing had changed. Jews, Judaism, anti-Semitism, they really didn't want to know anything about that. In their opinion the new government of Israel was as bad as fascism. Galinski, the head of the Jewish Community of Berlin, was nothing but a right-wing

We the Living Dead of This Land

extremist, so why question one's attitude toward anti-Semitism? And again and again the mendacious logic: we are the Left, and by definition leftists can't be anti-Semites. Without my being consciously aware of it, these experiences made me feel more and more Jewish, a Jewish woman who no longer had to keep on hiding and who didn't know exactly why she was different from the others. These experiences strengthened me, but even though I became more self-assured I also was affected by my continuous confrontation with the past. Jewishness for me here in Germany became a constant reminder of death and persecution and of a people that had changed very little if at all. Perhaps the way I looked also played a part, but I provoked others, regardless of where I was, to talk about the subject. At that time I used to visit Vienna often, and on the train I would invariably meet elderly people, women and men, who talked about the Nazis, the Jews, and so on. It caught up with me, regardless of where I was, it assaulted me even when I didn't expect it. And quite innocently I would get involved in conversations with people—my janitor, for example, a disgusting man of over eighty, who assured me that things hadn't been so bad for the Jews, or the woman on the train who immediately told me about all the people she had helped. In a bar, a restaurant, at the table next to mine, in the subway, wherever I happened to find myself, I was always on the alert, and then it would happen. Someone would say something stupid and I would be through for the day, would begin to swallow hard and keep on swallowing. I went to the theater to see Mehring's *The Merchant of Berlin*. The Jewish protagonist comes from the East with only $100 in his pocket and becomes stinking rich. But the worst part about it was the actor. They stuck *peyes* on him, dressed him in a black caftan, and make him look like a *Stürmer* stereotype. He didn't know a word of Yiddish and affected some dumb accent that had nothing to do with Yiddish. They put what was supposed to be a Jew on the stage and turned the whole thing into mockery. A play meant to be a piece of social criticism became a display of bad taste. No one noticed, and I was so furious I could have screamed. But all I did was cry silently to myself. And during the intermission all the chic people stood around, and I heard a beautiful, well-coiffed, bejeweled woman say, "Strange, the language these Jews speak."

In the feminist movement as well I came across tendencies that made me uncomfortable. Many of them tried to gain new insight into the history of women in the Third Reich. All of a sudden that League of German Girls ideology didn't seem so bad anymore. After all, didn't it get them away from home and onto their bicycles? Women among themselves. And then some women's magazines began to write about the "positive elements" in the League, that one mustn't put all the blame on women, they had also had a hard time, what with being alone, the men gone, they had to do everything themselves, had to be the men of the house. This turned into a very nasty trend toward absolution. Forgotten were the starry-eyed girls gazing at the Fuehrer, the guards in the women's camps, the mass of female Nazi voters, everything was as though it had never been.

They were brave, our mothers, they wrote, and we shouldn't say bad things about them. What the feminists didn't grasp was that by saying that, they were launching a general reconciliation with their parents. Understanding was replacing not only contempt but also criticism. Everything suddenly became understandable, and thus excusable. They began to single out the experiences of an individual mother or grandmother from the totality of events. My mother had to wash the diapers in cold water, meat was scarce, they had to go to the farmer for under-the-counter food. Fantastic, eh? But damn it, they sent their children to war, hailed a criminal, and looked on while other mothers were gassed or in other ways murdered. These German women didn't lift a finger against it. But worse was still to come. Some female journalists suddenly discovered there were others besides Jews who were put in concentration camps. Above all, other women. And they wrote articles, one of which began something like this: "When the prostitutes, lesbians, and Jewish women were being driven from their homes," and so forth.

It was now becoming clear: we women had always been persecuted, regardless of whether we were Jews, lesbians, prostitutes, or leftists. That writer equated herself with my murdered grandmother to assume the pose of victim. The whole article was written in a pseudo-Yiddish jargon and a loose, disgusting style that was enough to make you puke. Naturally it appeared in a left-wing journal. And it contained a sentence about a song the mothers sang to their sons before being gassed . . . So, you see, not a neo-Nazi tabloid making fun of the victims, but left-wing journalists in left-wing papers writing garbage like this. No one with a shred of decency could have written that sentence. They were standing in the gas chambers, these Yiddish mothers, their sons in their arms, and sang Yiddish songs to them. I could have screamed.

These ludicrous efforts of this generation trying with all their might to hide the fact that they are the descendants of the criminals. They stand in front of the closet that hides the skeleton and cry and whine and hope that this will dissuade people from looking into the closet.

Germans are often referred to as Mr. Normal Consumer. At times we have changed that to Mr. Normal Gasser. In their dealings with Jews they often feel the need to make themselves into victims. Occasionally Right and Left react identically.

I often feel that the Jews here in Germany are like the living dead. I once tried to make a connection between Dracula and the Jews. The Nazis had used figures from horror films as models in anti-Jewish pictures and exploited the fear of a strange being, the epitome of evil.

For centuries the Jews have had to defend themselves against the charge that they abduct and kill young girls to use their blood for ceremonial purposes. Dracula did the same. He had to suck the blood of young girls to keep on living. He couldn't help himself; he had to keep doing it to stay alive. There are pictures of him lying in his coffin, dead but not really dead, like the dead Jew who keeps on wandering around here. And the people were in fear of Dracula, closed the windows when he approached and were afraid to speak his name. They had to find a brave youth willing to drive a stake through Dracula's heart. Today, in the twentieth century, that can be done technologically. No test of courage is required. It's a matter of organization and systems. Machines take on the task of liberating the world from monsters like Dracula. The technically perfect murder machine of the Nazis was only a beginning, a trial run.

12

Mario

The Continuation of a Tragedy

MY LIFE, at least up to now, has been a tragedy, or rather the continuation of a tragedy that began fifty years ago, and the end is not in sight. I am now twenty-five. I was born in 1959, twenty-five years after the events in Germany, but my father's tragedy has become mine. My twin brother was damaged even more severely and is now undergoing psychiatric treatment. But what am I supposed to do? Blame my father for what he had to go through? He prepared his sons very badly for life in today's Germany, he turned us into living documentation, into a warning never to forget. But can that form the basis of life, of this the only life we have?

He came to Germany from Czechoslovakia as a young child after World War I, the son of a tailor. My father was one of six children. The family was among the poorest in the Jewish quarter. But as he often told me, my father refused to accept this poverty as his lot in life. He had no desire to follow the traditions of his parents, and as a youth he drank in the cultural life of the time. He didn't have any money, yet he still managed to go to the theater and the opera as often as possible. He became politically active, marched in demonstrations, and the like. He was fascinated by the assimilated, left-wing intellectual Jews of the twenties and early thirties, but also by everything German. The orderliness, cleanliness, and drive of this mixed German-Jewish culture became his ideal. That was the world he wanted to enter.

That's all I know about his family background. Questions were never asked; everything I know I've pieced together from casual remarks. All I know about his father is his trade, nothing more. That's all he ever told us about his family. They were all killed; he was the only one who saved himself. Neither his parents nor his five sisters survived the Nazis. But he never talked about what his family was like before that, before the Nazis came. The past was sacred, but not in a positive way. Like the word *Holocaust*, the past produced a feeling of anxiety in me, the fear of having touched on something forbidden. I know much more about the years of persecution. Of that he spoke often, perhaps even too often.

He was arrested once in the 1930s and then released. But that was all the warning he needed, and he fled to Poland a few days before the outbreak of the war. His parents and sisters stayed behind and he never saw them again.

When that happened he was younger than I am now, and he ran for his life, leaving behind everything that meant protection, warmth, and security. If I were to find myself in such a situation today, I don't think I could be as decisive. As far back as I can remember, my brother and I were brought up never to forget that we were surrounded by enemies. Yet in the event of overt, life-threatening aggression against me, I wouldn't know what to do. When the Germans marched into Poland, my father fled a second time. Together with a friend who now lives in Israel, he got to Rumania, where they were arrested by the fascist militia. That put an end to his flight as well as to the life he had known. They took away not only his freedom but also his optimism, his joy, and perhaps even his ability to love.

He was shipped to a concentration camp. Only God knows how he survived. Every day brought thousands of reasons and possibilities for dying and at most one for surviving, but he survived. It can't only have been sheer luck. His courage is his strength. He's not afraid of anybody. When it's a matter of principle he takes on anyone, whether it's a school director, a council member, or a mayor. Fear of authority is unknown to him. At the time in question he even managed to get himself transferred from the concentration camp to a slave-labor camp.

To me all stories about the war years are like paradoxical, completely illogical coincidences. Regardless of how often I listen to the story of his flight, of his life in the camp, it remains totally inconceivable, horrendous, and inhuman. Even his survival was inhuman. But my brother and I were constantly admonished with these tales. We were told never to forget and never to forgive. That is the most important legacy of my father. In Rumania he learned that his entire family had been murdered. A big family was simply gone, sunk like a ship without a trace. My father was the only one to survive. He got off in time and had to stand by helplessly while all the others drowned.

From that moment on he hated everything German. His life was defined by his desire for vengeance. When the Russians liberated his camp, he volunteered for the Russian army in order to fight against the Germans. He was wounded, lost part of his left leg, and spent the rest of the war in a hospital in the Caucasus.

His helpless rage about what the Germans had done to him,

together with his disappointment—for he had been proud to be a German—marked all his actions after the war. My brother and I grew up in an atmosphere of hatred, fear of a possible recurrence, and an insatiable need for vengeance.

Yet I think that when the war ended, while he was still in the Soviet Union, my father had a will to live. For example, he told us that in Moscow he again started to go to the theater and the opera. But he didn't stay in the Soviet Union long. Since he was a member of the Red Army's Czech brigade, he went to Prague, and from there he fled to Bavaria, back to Germany. He didn't return like other emigrants; he had to flee to the country that he had once fled to save his life. When I later asked him why he returned, given his contempt for this country, he said that he wanted to look for possible survivors of his family. But he already knew that they had all been murdered. All he found here was official confirmation. From then on his only purpose in life was to destroy everything that was nationalist German, anti-Semitic, and National Socialist.

That's when he met my mother, a blonde, blue-eyed, non-Jewish German woman. I have often asked myself how a Jew who had suffered so much could marry a blonde, blue-eyed German so soon after the war. What made him do it? After all, he hadn't come to Germany to forgive. If he had, I could understand this marriage as a symbol of reconciliation and an affirmation of life. I find many of his actions incomprehensible, but whose fault is that, his or mine?

My mother subordinated herself to my father from the very outset. She came of a liberal Protestant family, and perhaps she looked on this marriage as an act of expiation and restitution. Her sole concern was my father. Their emotional life was like an uncharted area on a map. My parents came to one another like friend and enemy, like victim and persecutor; they wanted to

The Continuation of a Tragedy

make a fresh start in a new Germany, one in which the past must never be forgotten or repeated. They measured whatever was happening in postwar Germany by the yardstick of the past. They didn't live in the present and had no positive feelings about the future. They decided that's how they wanted to live their lives, and no one has the right to blame them. But in that case why have children? Why bring into the world a new life that doesn't have a future and is doomed from the outset? Vengeance must always be guided by the past, and to bring children into the world to avenge the past was bound to end in tragedy.

My brother and I were born in 1959. Although we were born in Germany, nothing about us was allowed to be German. We were given Italianate names, and even though our mother wasn't Jewish we were bar mitzvah'd. My father succeeded in having us admitted into the Jewish Community. All they asked was that my mother leave the church. We also didn't have German citizenship or German passports. My father had refused to reclaim his German citizenship, and my mother relinquished hers. All of us are stateless foreigners, even though we were born here and have lived here for decades.

My passport states that the bearer is a stateless foreigner. A German bureaucrat sitting in a government office has certified that I am homeless, that I am not at home anywhere, that I belong nowhere. Lately this document has become a hindrance to me. I need a visa for every country I visit, and some socialist countries don't accept it at all since they suspect the bearer of being a refugee from Eastern Europe. I have to explain to every consular official how I came to have such a passport and that my father was persecuted by the Nazis. This ID stamps me. Wherever I travel I carry my father's sorrow with me in the form of a document.

My father says that he owes it to his murdered relatives never to become a German. Okay, one can't argue with that, but then why live here in Germany? As important as my Jewishness now is to me, I don't think that I would ever insist that my children should also be Jewish. Or if I did, I wouldn't live with them in Germany.

When we were little the problem of living as a Jew in Germany did not loom large for my brother and me. For a while we even attended a Catholic kindergarten, and at home we celebrated only the most important Jewish holidays. But when we began school everything changed. The idea that we were different was injected into us, not so much as a religious consciousness or the feeling of being part of a community but as the mark of a persecuted minority in a hostile environment. My father's hysterical mistrust of his neighbors isolated us children completely.

We led the lives of segregated freaks, not allowed to play with other children, to invite or visit friends, to go outside our house by ourselves—no playground, no street games with other boys, no stopping for hot dogs, no ice cream after school, nothing. My mother tried to make up for all this. We had a little house with a garden, and there we played, painted pictures, puttered around, but always only the three of us. We were like Siamese twins who are never alone yet always lonely.

In school the other kids avoided us. Nobody liked us or came near us. At recess we stood alone in a corner eating our sandwiches while the others ran around and had fun. We were defensive and unfeeling and didn't want to join in with the others. My mother never actually demanded any of this, but it was etched into us like a law, a law that was obeyed by my mother and by us. And there was no back talk.

My mother forbade us to walk home from school with other

The Continuation of a Tragedy

kids even if they were neighbors. We were like little robots, quiet, helpful, reserved, obedient.

And if Jewishness by itself wasn't enough to stamp us as outsiders, we were brought up to make clear to everybody that we did not belong and never would belong. Most people could not imagine the hatred with which the others reacted to that. We also made ourselves unpopular in other ways. Since we had been told at home never to lie, always to do what's right, and since the other kids in the class were by definition evil, we reported anyone who broke a rule or copied homework. And when we told them at home how unpopular this made us, we were praised for having done the right thing and told that the others were bad. Our antisocial behavior was supported by our parents. It almost seemed as if they wanted to keep us in isolation as long as possible.

As time went on, things got worse for us children. We were called names, naturally including anti-Semitic slurs. The tone became more and more aggressive. Some even went so far as to say they wouldn't mind a new anti-Jewish campaign if that would get rid of us. But in fact we practically asked for it. Through us our classmates came to feel my father's hatred and they hit back, perhaps with their fathers' hatred. But they were hitting us, a generation that can be said to have the good fortune not to have experienced the horrors of the war.

Of course we told our parents what was happening at school, and that always led to a big blow-up. My father would go to the principal and demand the expulsion of certain pupils and even of some teachers. They would then be called to the principal, and the upshot was that they hated us even more, and we withdrew even more.

My father seemed to thrive on making these complaints. He

shouted and he insulted them, and most of the time he got his way. We were a part of his vengeance, his personal vendetta. But was it worth it? Was it worth sacrificing the children to ferret out old or new persecutors? At the time I thought he was wrong, but today I can't blame him for it. He is just as much a victim as my brother and I, and certainly he has gone through much more. But the question I keep asking myself and for which there is no answer is this: Why did he really come back to Germany?

And all the time things in school kept getting worse. We were thirteen, our hair was cut very short, our neatly buttoned white shirts were tucked into gray pants, while the others dressed in colorful outfits, wore their hair long, and began to go out with girls. For us that was unthinkable. I didn't buy my first pair of jeans until I was twenty. But slowly I stopped taking for granted everything I was told at home. I was a fish out of water. I didn't know the rules of soccer and didn't understand my classmates' dirty jokes. We were like marionettes, nothing spontaneous, nothing unpremeditated. Then, when I was fourteen, my parents for the first time let me go on a skiing trip with my class, and there something strange happened. I broke a leg and had to go to the hospital. For the first time I was alone, separated from my brother and my parents, but my classmates who up to then had shunned me came to see me, brought me a radio, were friendly and tried to console me. I was on top of the world. People no longer seemed hostile; on the contrary, they were helpful, caring, and compassionate. From that day on I stopped taking my mother's rules and warnings so seriously. I also began to let my schoolwork slip, and I fell in love for the first time, with a Turkish girl.

But my brother kept on getting worse. He said the teachers were part of a network of conspirators working with German

The Continuation of a Tragedy

intelligence or the CIA. He wrote it all down. When people came near him, he would squint and his face took on a tight, anxious look. He hated everything American and even went so far as to say there was a conspiracy against him and that he might have to escape to East Germany or the Soviet Union.

My mother talked to him for hours on end, and he would shout at her hysterically, his eyes popping, his face beet-red. Sometimes this would go on all night, while my father stood outside the door and listened without intervening. The neighbors began to talk. I had the feeling that I was surrounded by insanity. That's when I began to turn away from Judaism. I couldn't stand observing the Sabbath and didn't feel like going to synagogue.

Somehow my brother and I managed to finish high school. My brother wanted to study art but was rejected by two of the schools he applied to. Again my father protested, saying that he was rejected only because he was Jewish. Meanwhile my brother was getting worse and worse. I finally persuaded him to see a neurologist. My own situation, however, improved. I got my own apartment, and I began my studies. I also became more involved with things Jewish, joined the Jewish student organization, and for a time I was even a member of the executive committee.

Recently I applied for German citizenship. This summer I plan to go to Israel and work on a kibbutz. I am looking forward to meeting the people, to the positive feeling of building something jointly with them. But I don't want to emigrate. I want to live here in Germany and finish my studies. As a German and a Jew I believe I have the right to live and study here. At one time I also consulted a doctor, but it wasn't a good experience. A psychiatrist once advised me to renounce my Judaism, what with my mother being German. I don't know how he thinks it can be done. Should I throw it off like dirty underwear in order to become clean?

I now believe that I can make a go of it. And once I've finished college and am earning enough money I also want to take care of my brother. But for the time being I have to concentrate on myself. I visit my parents only rarely. I try to live without forgetting my father's misfortune yet without letting it become mine. It isn't easy to develop such a positive attitude here in Germany, but I think I'll succeed. Because on one point I agree with my father: nothing has changed. To rid Germany of Jews they had to collect them, ship them off, and murder them. But to become de-Nazified all they had to do was to say "Good morning" instead of "Heil Hitler" when they picked up their breakfast rolls at the bakery.

13

Aaron

We Jews Pray, We Don't Beg

MY NAME IS AARON. I and my family live in Berlin. So do my parents and my father's brother. We come from an old Berlin family, Orthodox Jews who've lived here for generations. That probably explains why my parents came back to Berlin after the war. Nothing anybody said could deter them. They felt that this was where they belonged. Not that they necessarily felt that this was their country or their city. I don't even know whether they think of themselves as Germans; that issue doesn't seem too important to them. However, they believe that you leave when you have to leave, and that you return when the time is right.

Returning, coming back and beginning anew, is after all one of the powerful forces of the Jewish tradition. Over the centuries Jews have been returning to the very places that have been the scenes of their suffering and persecution. They rebuilt what had been destroyed, and through their courage proved that their faith was stronger than all their suffering.

I'm not particularly grateful to my parents for coming back to Germany and bringing me up here. I won't go so far as to say that I'm trying to prove something by living in this extreme situation—for living here in Germany as an Orthodox Jew is indeed an odd situation. My family and I don't wish to be seen as living testimony that Hitler did not chalk up a total victory in his war against the Jews. No person of any religious faith, and certainly not we Jews, should want to become this kind of symbol. Anyone who does should change his religion.

It is as normal for Jews to live in Germany today as it is for Jews to live in Spain today. Not that I'm equating extermination and exile. Tragedies have never been the building blocks of our people. We've known the Holocaust, the Crusades, the pogroms in Russia and Poland. Each group of barbaric persecutors and murderers came up with its own technique. Who's to decide that one or the other method was so heinous that Jews can no longer live among its perpetrators. That they cannot come back and start all over again? It's not up to me to judge whether a particular political system is or is not safe for Jews. How often have the Jews thought that at last they had come to a country where they could live in peace? And how often have they been wrong?

My life is based on mitzvah, nothing else. Anything else is a joke, a sheer waste of time. Would I still be an Orthodox Jew today if my forefathers hadn't stood by their religion in the face of indescribable difficulties and under all sorts of conditions? Was the Holocaust really so unprecedented as to give Jews the world over the right to condemn other Jews for returning to live in Germany? Would there be any Jews left at all if our forefathers had felt that way? I don't want to criticize those Jews who are happy not to be living in Germany. But they shouldn't turn up their noses at us, they should support us. Besides, and this may sound cynical, Jews have lived in peace for relatively long periods in countries that had seen dreadful pogroms during their lifetime. Anyway, I'm proud to live with my family in Germany, as a religious Jew.

Not all my relatives have always been Orthodox. A few of them tried their best to become assimilated. And they were proved wrong. In the end, they were left with nothing, not even with the one anchor they could have taken with them when they fled—their religion. Something that happened in my grandfather's family is a case in point. My grandfather's brother volunteered for the army in World War I, much against the wishes of his parents, devout Jews. He was a brave soldier, yet he wasn't promoted, didn't get a commission—I'm not sure of the details. In any case, during the war he converted and then was made an officer. He came back home proud of his contribution to the lost war, his chest full of medals, feeling fully a part of the German people. He had lost all interest in Judaism. As far as he was concerned, assimilation was the solution to the Jewish problem. In 1937, my father together with his parents and other relatives left Germany, but this uncle—Leo by name—refused to join them. He run away? An honored, decorated officer of the Prussian army? From whom? No amount of urging by relatives and friends could change his mind. He was convinced that nothing could happen to him. Yet he was one of the first they took away. He had completely ignored all the regulations applying to Jews. Since he didn't consider himself a Jew he refused to act like one. He was killed in a concentration camp, I don't even know which one. And his decorations? Maybe some guard took them. Had they burned him in full uniform, those medals might have remained in the ashes. Anyhow, they certainly didn't help my uncle survive. What a horror. I can hardly bear to think of how his recklessness brought tragedy not only to him but also to his family. During World War I, 12,000 Jewish soldiers were killed, out of a total of 500,000 German Jews. That was a higher percentage than the non-Jewish casualties. One wonders how many German Jews would have gone along with Hitler if he hadn't been an anti-Semite.

My parents went to Palestine. In the early 1950s they came back to Berlin. I was born in Tel Aviv in 1948, and I can hardly remember anything before Berlin. I wasn't the one who decided to live in Germany. I'm here because of my parents. Still, the morning prayer is the same whether you wake up in Berlin or Jerusalem. So there is no wrong place to live according to God's laws. And when devout Jews gathered in secret to pray in the concentration camps, I believe that even there they didn't beg for their lives. "So may it be Thy will," the prayer says. Unlike the Christians, I think we don't formally implore God to hear our pleas. And we offer the same prayer wherever we may be. So where we live is not all that important, except perhaps for Israel, and even that doesn't make such a big difference.

I went to school in Berlin and studied medicine there. My life as a young man in Berlin was as ordinary as anyone else's. There was no anti-Semitism, no derision, no stupid remarks, no jokes. I'm afraid I can't be of any help to those who are forever talking about the resurgence of anti-Semitism. I haven't experienced it, and I'm not afraid of a possible recurrence of what happened during the Third Reich.

At any rate, fifteen years after the persecution of the Jews I attended school here as a small boy, and perhaps even had a teacher who earlier had preached hatred of the Jews. But my parents insisted on respect for our religious laws. Of course I didn't go to school on Saturdays or on Jewish holidays, and on school outings I didn't eat everything. I was often asked to tell the class how we celebrated the Sabbath and how I prepared for my bar mitzvah.

We once had a teacher who told my father that he thought I might profit from attending school on Saturday, when important subjects like mathematics and German were taught. He also thought it would make for greater camaraderie. Why should I be at a disadvantage, and so on.

My father simply asked him whether math and German were more important than the study of the Torah, and whether class spirit was more crucial to my development than sharing the Sabbath with my family? I don't think the teacher quite understood my father, but he never again brought up the subject.

At home too we lived as Orthodox Jews. Berlin has everything: synagogues, kosher butchers, whatever is needed.

My parents are simple people. They didn't go to college and become professionals. What they know they learned from their parents, from various rabbis, and on their own. Nor has my father ever held any official position in the Community. That's not for him. He believes that it would divert him from the real task of serving God. But it was precisely their simple modesty that made me want to emulate my parents. They gave me self-confidence, a sense of identity that I find lacking in most Jews in Germany. Am I a German, or a Jew? Or am I first a German, and then a Jew? What quibbling nonsense, what a waste of time. I prefer to spend my time with my books.

My parents taught me how to practice my religion even in an isolated situation, and I try to pass this on to my four children. Two are of school age; two are still in kindergarten. The family is their strongest support, and I impress this on them. Maybe this wouldn't be so critical in another country, but here, where my children have very few Jewish friends simply because there are so few Jews, home and the support of the family take on special importance.

My wife, my children, my parents, my wife's parents—these are the most important people in my life. Nothing else matters as much. My children attended the Jewish kindergarten. To my regret there is no Jewish grade school. But my wife and I, and of course the grandparents, try to give the children at least a minimal religious education. I see that as my most important responsibility. I'm not involved in any committees championing Jewish causes or defending Jewish interests. I'd rather concentrate on the children. Word of what I'm doing has spread among other Jewish parents, and now some of them send their children to me for instruction. This is the real job of us Jews in Germany: passing the tradition on to our children. Being born of Jewish mothers does not make us special; that's not enough. And I can't live the way so many Jews here in Germany do who see the persecution of their relatives in the Third Reich as both basis and proof of their vulnerable situation here. Why don't they come back to the rebuilt synagogues if their Jewish identity has suddenly become so important? Why do they rather talk about our murderers, about the synagogues that are still not rebuilt and the desecrated cemeteries, rather than about their religious beliefs? Why do they fight anti-Semitism when they have no faith? Are they freedom fighters or what? Okay, but why keep harping on the Jewish tradition when they don't live it?

There are plenty of synagogues in Germany, maybe even too many to judge by how many of them stand empty. If only half of the politically or socially involved Jews in Germany would invest that much energy in the religious communities, things would be different today. Everybody knows that the successful producer Peter Zadek is a Jew. But how many can identify even one rabbi?

We Jews Pray, We Don't Beg

It would be nice if well-known Jews like Zadek would support the founding of a Jewish school. That would do more for Judaism in Germany than being a celebrity in the arts. Above all we here, the children of the survivors, have a religious responsibility. Everything else is nostalgia and coy manipulation of prejudice. Our sorrow over the horrors of the Nazi era belongs in our prayers, not in front of microphones. We've got to stop yelling every time we hear of any anti-Semitic stupidity. We're seen either as persecutors in the form of Israeli soldiers or as victims, survivors or their children. A dubious identity.

During Sukkoth I build a tabernacle on my balcony. It's a symbol, but the children enjoy it, and maybe they'll do the same when they have children. In the past I've often invited Jewish friends with their children. They always enjoyed coming, they celebrated with us, and it's always been very festive. But later when I asked these same people whether they had celebrated the festival themselves, they'd become evasive. They forgot, didn't think of it, had no time—stupid, lame excuses or sheer ignorance.

But talk alone won't do any good. If we don't perpetuate the religious tradition, it will soon be over with the Jews in Germany. Our communities have to do more than just react to stupidity and violence. This doesn't mean closing our eyes to reality. Quite the contrary. We need help. As parents we need help with the education of our children. Because sometimes I have the feeling that we're not making it, not even in my own family. As traditional Jews our children are exotic plants in this German forest. They bear the tremendous burden of being outsiders, even of isolation and lack of understanding. It is not always easy for us parents to give them the strength they need, even when they have been brought up in a traditional home.

But emigration is not an alternative, at least not for me. And where would we go? Our lives couldn't be any more devout in Israel than they are here. There are no two categories of Jews. The Jewish faith does not endow people with any kind of divinity. Jews can live anywhere on earth as they see fit according to the laws and find God. They need no intermediaries, no Jewish officials or banknotes with Hebrew lettering.

Quite frankly, my wife and I don't see eye to eye on this. I think she wouldn't mind if we left. But she has other reasons as well. She comes from Italy, from a big Jewish family, and is used to being part of a large circle. The biggest problem she has here is the loneliness, the isolation, the fact that there are only a few Jewish families, that we have very few contacts with other Jews, and almost none with non-Jews. She came here to study German and literature. I met her on the way to the synagogue, when she stopped me to ask for directions. The last thing I expected was to meet a Jewish girl from Italy, and in Berlin of all places. But she also comes from a family where hate was never advocated. She had always wanted to study German literature and so her family sent her to Germany. When she told her parents about me, they were surprised to hear that she had met a Jewish young man here in Germany and wanted to marry him. I think she would really like us to go to Italy. But what would I do there? I'm a physician, I work in a hospital, and we have a decent income. What would I do in Italy?

So we too have this running discussion in our family, whether to leave or stay. I'm almost forty. My children are growing up here and like it here. They speak German, have German friends, and live normal lives as Jews, with far fewer problems than our generation had. Why should I leave?

Of course, it's wonderful to visit my wife's family, when thirty or forty people get together, all of them family, to see four generations sit at one table, the ninety-year-olds together with the infants. I must admit I find it extremely moving. It's also wonderful for the children. We generally spend our summers there. I often think about the time when my parents were children here in Germany. It must have been very similar for them then. But that was a long time ago. Today we Jews in Germany are in a peculiar position. We're often thrown together with other minorities, even though we speak German and didn't just arrive here, like the Italians and the Turks. How often have people told me, on hearing that I was Jewish, that they have stood up for their Turkish neighbors. How often have I had a doctor tell me that he has treated refugees free of charge. They want to demonstrate their solidarity, their understanding of persecuted people, and they don't realize that by doing that they're again making me into an outsider. I'm being pushed into the role of victim, yet I don't feel persecuted nor is there any actual reason why I should.

My son once brought a school friend home on his birthday. The boy looked at everything in the house and I asked him if he would like to visit on one of our holidays. We invited him for Hanukkah. The boy was very interested, very open, and asked many questions. Because everything went so well, we once also invited his parents, and they came. But the conversation dragged on. I asked this and that, they answered politely, but they themselves didn't ask me anything. They were nervous and uncomfortable, and I had the feeling they couldn't wait to leave. It isn't easy for my children, having so little contact with Germans. There is always a wall of silence and uneasiness between us and them. That's not necessarily a sign of anti-Semitism or prejudice. On the contrary, many Germans harbor feelings of guilt that make it hard for them to approach us Jews, even harder than it is for us to approach them. But it's still a difficult problem for me.

AARON

I try to live here in Germany as though the past is not forgotten yet still not part of everyday life. But for my generation that's very difficult, almost impossible. However, as far as the children are concerned, Jewish and non-Jewish, I have hope. Maybe future generations will live together more freely and openly. I have a kind of vision of my children and my children's children, living here as traditional, devout Jews, together with Jewish and non-Jewish friends. And I am devoting all my energy to the realization of this dream. It is perhaps the motivating force of my life. In this my wife and I are in agreement; it's what we both wish for.

I don't want my children to be considered victims. I don't want their lives overshadowed by pity or misguided understanding based on feelings of guilt.

My generation was planted here like seedlings in poisoned soil. Putting out religious roots has not been easy. It has been challenging. When I first came to the hospital, my colleagues knew nothing about Jewish customs and religion, and there were things they couldn't understand—for example, why I insisted on taking off on Rosh Hashanah and didn't mind working on Christmas. But today they accept and respect my way of life. And even my generation of non-Jews is beginning to find life among us Jews normal.

Nevertheless we have to remain alert. After all, vigilance saved my parents' lives. My parents are both at home now. My father had worked for many years in a textile mill, while my mother took care of the family. They are neither rich nor poor. They have enough to live on, and they don't plan to leave the country again.

It's good for my children to know grandparents. How many in my generation grew up without any relatives at all. Simon Wiesenthal tells how he once asked a friend to pretend to be his daughter's uncle, because the little girl had asked him why she wasn't like the other children in her class, who all had relatives. This is the real drama of young Jews in Germany. Hatred robbed them of the warmth and security of large families. Today, two generations later, my children at least have a small family; they have parents and grandparents. Should I destroy this slow rebirth of a Jewish community and homeland here in Germany by fleeing when there's no good reason to do so? I'd like to see the Jew who can tell me to do just that and still in good conscience go to synagogue Friday evening. I intend to stay here with my family.

14

Peter S.

Postscript to My Life

WHAT KINDS of people are these? What makes them live here? What do they have in common? In what ways do they suffer? How do their parents' experiences color their lives? Questions, questions, questions I am asked over and over again when I talk about this book, about young Jews in Germany and Austria. And I find it difficult to give answers. It is impossible to condense into a sentence or two what I myself experienced during my conversations with the children of survivors here in Germany and in Austria, with these women, men, and young people who spent many hours with me talking about their parents, relatives, and friends, about their families and about themselves.

I sat and listened, only rarely interrupting them with questions, and as they talked I would forget the tape recorder and even the book that I was planning. The experiences, memories, fantasies, and yearnings of my subjects were journeys into my own past and that of my parents and relatives. And if there was anything that was identical in all these conversations, it was my own, recurrent reaction: for God's sake, that's just the way it was for me.

Even if all of us in this book are different, from different backgrounds and with different ideas about how and where we want to live, one thing unites us, whether we like it or not—our common past. We don't have a common future, but the horrors of the Nazi era, the survival of our own parents, the death of so many others, create a bond we cannot sever, regardless of whether we now consider ourselves Orthodox, observant, pious Jews or assimilated German or Austrian Jews who do not feel like Jews.

The images from these interviews haunted me. They reminded me of the experiences of my parents and the death of their families. They would not let me rest and fixed themselves in my head as pictures of a cruel death—in the gas chamber, in the cattle train, under the whip of an Austrian or German. They were always with me, like a projection slide implanted in my skull.

My parents survived.

My father was sixteen when he, his older brother, and two friends decided to leave without their parents. They squirreled away provisions, and one day, long after the Germans had marched into Austria, they left without saying good-bye. Traveling from Vienna through Germany—their passport stamped with that indelible "J"—they reached the Belgian border, and there they were arrested. In the middle of the night a man came to their prison cell, put them in a car, drove them to some woods, and, pointing into the darkness toward Belgium, told them to scram. Their savior—a Gestapo officer.

My father's parents remained behind. My grandfather died

some months later, before being deported. My grandmother and her young daughter went into hiding in Vienna, but ultimately they were denounced and taken away. My father never saw them again.

My mother, who lived in Prague, left for London ten days before the German invasion, a phony baptismal certificate and the invitation of an English family safely in her pocket. Her mother stayed behind. Her father had died two years earlier. Even though her mother had all the necessary papers for emigration, she stayed in Prague taking care of two children whose parents had already left and who were going to send for them once they had the requisite papers. But it was too late. For all of them. My grandmother and her two charges were taken to Theresienstadt. She worked there as a nurse and then accompanied the two children to Auschwitz. As a nurse she could have stayed in Theresienstadt and perhaps might even have survived, but she chose to look after two children who were not her own.

I was born in Vienna only two years later, in 1947. What crime have I committed that I had to grow up without grandparents, without aunts and uncles or any other relatives? What did I do to make my mother break into tears whenever I asked about my grandmother?

My parents survived—my father as a soldier in the British army, my mother as a nurse in London. Two people, almost the only members of two large families, managed to escape through a fluke, a flaw in the system, through the treason of a Gestapo man who saved my father and the treason of a priest who secured a baptismal certificate for my mother. I was born into this world because two people did not obey the rules. That is the basis of my existence.

At that point my thinking becomes blocked, all logic ceases. All efforts to understand the past, to rid myself of it, to detach myself so that I can forget or at least repress it, turn into a desperate and to me a frequently ludicrous effort. And that's why there is no reconciliation for me and never can be. This mass murder, committed by one mass of people against another, cannot be explained by anything that would make reconciliation possible.

As long as I have known about the past, I have lived with my back against the wall, as have many others of my generation. Because if we children of the victims of the Nazis have something in common, it is the almost sacred duty this time, the next time, to get out in time. The fear that we will miss the right moment, the moment when we are still able to save ourselves, is our biggest and perhaps even our only fear. That theme came up in every one of the conversations, as though the murdered victims were swearing us to vigilance.

Escape has become the most important theme of my life and also of the lives of most of those who appear in this book. It manifests itself in the most varied fantasies and modes of behavior. One person dreams of acquiring as many passports and nationalities as possible, another buys suitcases, others refuse to own property in Germany or Austria, and still others judge their non-Jewish friends by whether they think they'd hide them or not. What drives us to these fantasies is not so much the fear of death, but the rage and despair over what happened. They must not succeed again. We will never again allow ourselves to ignore the first warnings, to think that it can't happen again.

But the next generation is very different. Our children feel at home here, consider themselves Germans or Austrians and are frightened of having to leave here. They speak of their friends, are proud of their country, and many of them would rather go into hiding in the case of a resurgent anti-Semitism, even give up their rituals and synagogues, if only they don't have to leave this newly won home. They cannot imagine that Austria and Germany could again mount an organized extermination of the Jews. That is where they differ from us.

Almost all the interviewees of my generation, me included, believe the people of Austria and Germany are capable of a repetition of those events. To expect the people of these two countries to feel guilt, and consequently to rule out the possibility of a recurrence, reflects a degree of naïveté we cannot afford.

There was no guilt-ridden awakening among the Germans after 1945, let alone among the Austrians. The mass murder of the Jews and the preceding daily terror was a reality planned and executed by more than a hundred thousand bureaucrats. The fairy tale of individual criminals and the innocence of all others is so inane that it doesn't even qualify as a fairy tale.

William Shirer, who was in Vienna when the Germans marched into that city, had this to say about the behavior of those friendly, kind, genial Viennese:

> For the first few weeks the behavior of the Vienna Nazis was worse than anything I had seen in Germany. There was an orgy of sadism. Day after day large numbers of Jewish men and women could be seen scrubbing Schuschnigg signs off the sidewalk and cleaning the gutters. While they worked on their hands and knees with jeering storm troopers standing over them, crowds gathered to taunt them. Hundreds of Jews, men and women, were picked off the streets and put to work cleaning public latrines and the toilets of the barracks where the S.A. and the S.S. were quartered. Tens of thousands more were jailed. Their worldly possessions were confiscated or stolen. . . .*

Our ideas about good and evil, our naïve expectations of humanitarian behavior and humaneness, were answered by the gas

* William L. Shirer, *The Rise and Fall of the Third Reich* (New York: Simon and Schuster, 1960), 351.

ovens. For hundreds of years the Jews sought to impose a humane face on the German-speaking cultural sphere. They paid for it with their lives. For hundreds of years they tried to help these two peoples, whose history showed them to be far inferior to other civilized European cultures, to become mature. But those malicious children killed their teachers, destroyed their schools, and returned to collective barbarism. Perhaps it was too early. But who would want to try again?

Of the many known facts about the very different way the people in the occupied territories reacted to the planned murder of the Jews, one fact—barely known in Austria and Germany—has impressed me more than any other. The Jews of Bulgaria were in part saved by the resistance of the population. Not only did they not participate in the persecution, they also did not allow their fellow citizens to be deported. They demonstrated en masse and ultimately prevented the extermination. Beckerle, the German ambassador to Bulgaria, sent the following cable to his government on 7 June, 1943:

> I am fully convinced that the Minister President and the government are working for the final solution of the Jewish question. But in that effort they are hindered by the mentality of the Bulgarian people, who lack the ideological enlightenment we possess. Having grown up with Armenians, Greeks, and gypsies, the Bulgarians don't find any flaws in the Jews that would justify special measures. . . .

Vienna and the major German cities like Berlin and Frankfurt had a Jewish population of 5 to 10 percent; Sofia had about 9 percent.

I am deeply impressed by the reaction of the Bulgarian people. Here in this country a law had to be passed threatening punitive measures against anyone who called Auschwitz a lie.

PETER S.

For the second time the state is intervening in the same matter: the first time to build and operate Auschwitz and the second time to punish those who claim it never existed. That's how the state protects its monuments.

I did not grow up a religious Jew. My Jewishness is not founded on the handing down of religious traditions. But several times when I was little I was awakened by the repeated ringing of the telephone. When my father didn't answer after the second or third ring and stayed in bed, I put on my slippers, went down the stairs, answered the phone, and heard a voice say, "Jewish swine." I didn't hang up right away, but stood there petrified, and the "Jewish swine" kept on ringing in my ears.

The proof of my Jewishness lies in the murder of my relatives and in anti-Semitism. I don't have the good fortune—and this word also encompasses my yearning—to be a believer. I have to turn to people with my worries, my fears, and my hopes. And I don't think too much of them. Most of the people among whom I live failed in their attempt to murder my parents but they succeeded with the others. The basis of my Jewishness therefore is a crime that unfortunately succeeded in most instances and failed only in very rare cases. And for that I cannot hold a higher authority responsible, cannot rely on punishment by God or some supreme being. A majority of barbaric, unfeeling people here in Germany and in Austria participated in or at least tolerated the murder without resisting.

But a person whose life is marked solely and exclusively by the past has no future. My future is the past, and therefore I have none. For in one respect Hitler and his people were victorious. The final solution did take place. The Jewish problem in Austria and Germany can be said to have been solved. We are not the remnant of a Lost World, as an exhibit about the Jews of Vienna was called, we are the sorry remnant of a scuttled world.

Postscript to My Life

Hatred, fury, pain, mourning, despair, and fear are the dominant feelings of the people with whom I spoke. But they all live their own story, often don't even understand each other, don't even think much of each other. But they have much in common in their feelings about the non-Jews here in Austria and Germany. The Germans and Austrians had wanted to kill their parents; every family has its victims; they live in the land of the murderers; and they are afraid that the next time they might not get out in time. These basic fears set them so far apart from everybody else that they are involuntarily brought together. What makes them feel like strangers in this country is not a superimposed communality, an irrational cultural behavior or closeness based on their background or the way they think, but the hopelessness—at least for my generation—of ever again looking on Germany and Austria as home.

Having grown up as a nonobservant Jew, without Jewish festivals and synagogue, I visited Auschwitz as a seventeen-year-old with a group of other students. And this trip tore me out of my lethargy and repression, awoke me from my sleep, recalled me to my background, as though a hot needle had been inserted under my skin that will never cool off until the day I die.

When I saw the concentration camp, the mass murders I knew about from books and films and the accounts of the older generation turned into the murder of my own relatives and therefore became intolerable. What I saw behind the glass wall of the museum was not a huge mountain of hair, eyeglasses, suitcases, and spoons but the hair of my grandmother, her suitcase, the glasses of my father's little sister. It was a visit to the scene of the crime, and I was looking at the remains of my relatives in order to identify them. Perhaps I shouldn't have gone there. Most people of my generation, as the children of the Nazi victims, have never been to a concentration camp. Many

Peter S.

of them cannot read books or see films about that time. But what I saw in Auschwitz were museum exhibits of the remains of my grandmother, of my aunts, uncles, and all the other relatives, the remnants of a culture I was no longer able to experience.

I was sitting in a park in Vienna with Aryeh, whose story appears in this book, on a wonderful, warm fall day. The leaves were turning. We were sitting on a bench, eyes closed, feeling the sun on our faces, the fading sun before winter begins. And in the midst of this idyll of light and color, Aryeh suddenly turned to me and said, It's crazy what they did to our people. Regardless of who we are, what we do, and what we are thinking about, it overcomes us, imposes itself on us, interrupts our thoughts and feelings.

And we develop a sensitivity those around us often cannot deal with. The increasing references to the persecution of Jews in the daily political discourse make me both angry and sad. Those who say that pacifism made Auschwitz possible and those who speak of an atomic holocaust are all guilty of an unfeeling use of language, and in the final analysis of a mockery of the Nazi victims.

In the various political camps a new attitude is developing that not only rejects embarrassment and guilt but doesn't even require consideration of the sensibilities of the few survivors and their children. More and more, guilt and complicity in murder and expulsion are becoming a historically conditioned, understandable, and explainable kind of behavior, divorced from individual accountability. Reverence is no longer demanded.

Even such liberal journals as *Die Zeit* are no exception. In an article of 10 October 1984 on restitution, a photo from a concentration camp was used as illustration. The caption read, "Corpses piled up in a concentration camp." I venture to say that whoever selected the picture did not expect to find his relatives among the bodies. But what I saw there wasn't a pile of corpses in a slaughterhouse but individuals, dead men and women lying on top of each other, emaciated bodies, skin and bones. And the third one from the left, the one with the wide-open eyes, was perhaps my . . .

A Berlin magazine in the fall of 1984 published a story about a pensioner who was not allowed to sit on a bench because the landlord wanted it for himself. Next to it was a drawing, a cartoon showing two benches. On the top one it said "Only for Aryans" and the date—1934. The caption on the bottom one read "Only for landlords" and the date—1984. This desperate effort to turn oneself into one of the victims, to dissociate from the murderers, to show that one had nothing to do with them, uses my murdered relatives to wash away the guilt.

Restitution forced the survivors to stand in line, pleading, so as to help the murderers do a good deed. It was not a compensation for the criminal act but a sop to the conscience of the criminal.

The conversations in this book were not interviews, not question-and-answer games. They were journeys into long-lost worlds, into the present, and occasionally also into the future. Some people were so relieved to be able to talk about this subject at last that the conversations turned into hour-long monologues. But others, and there were quite a number of them, refused to talk to me about it altogether, even about their fears. Some wanted to use their real names and others asked me to change their names and any other identifying features. All were different, yet none was alien to me. Frequently their stories led me to talk about myself or to laugh and cry with them because their stories were so much like my own or those of my relatives. Because every Jewish woman, every Jewish man, every Jewish child also was telling me about my own life. It was as though they were taking me by the hand. Every conversation turned into a long walk together.

The fact that this book is being written now, at this time, is no accident. And it is also no accident that these people cooperated so enthusiastically. We, as the oldest of the postwar generation of Jews, are almost forty years of age now, an age at which the search for one's past and roots grows stronger and stronger. We tried to overcome the vacuum into which we were born by looking toward various political and other groups to replace our lost home rather than to our own tradition. But they weren't substitutes, neither the Left of the late sixties nor the powerful economic interests who integrated us into their sphere. What we lack most of all today is an older generation. It must have been beautiful to have an old, wise generation to love and venerate and learn from. They were taken from us, we had to grow up without them. But we also lack contemporaries. So few of them are still around. And we often cling together because with the "others" everything is even more of a problem.

Recently I myself began to search for the roots that make up my being and my imagination. Most of all I was curious. I tried to acquire at least a minimum of Jewish learning, went to the synagogue with religious friends and was happy when I got invitations to Jewish holiday celebrations. Everything I did was influenced by a steadily growing feeling of awe.

Who am I, I now ask myself, to interrupt a more than five-thousand-year-old tradition? I will never get rid of the horror of the Nazis. The dead compel me to think and act in a certain way. I will always be a Jew, regardless of what I do. But more and more I feel compelled not only to accept this but also to dare trying to live as a Jew—whatever that may mean. Perhaps working on this book has also stirred a yearning in me, a yearning despite the sad past to live with a Jewish present and a Jewish

Postscript to My Life

future. Whether that is possible in Austria and Germany I don't know. I have tried to do it in both countries. Perhaps I have to find a new country if I want to live in peace. Or maybe an uneasy restlessness is the only tolerable alternative for me.